THE COMPLETE

ElfQuest®

THE COMPLETE ELFQUEST®

VOLUME THREE

BY WENDY AND RICHARD PINI

STORY BY

SARAH BYAM

(HIDDEN YEARS PART 9)

PENCILS BY

PAUL ABRAMS

(HIDDEN YEARS PARTS 8–9)

INKS BY

CHARLES BARNETT

(HIDDEN YEARS PARTS 8–9)

JOHN BYRNE

(HIDDEN YEARS PART 9½)

COLORS BY

PATY COCKRUM

(HIDDEN YEARS PARTS 8–9)

SUZANNE DECHNIK

(HIDDEN YEARS PART 9½)

LETTERS BY

GARY KATO

(HIDDEN YEARS PART 9)

LORINA MAPA

(HIDDEN YEARS PART 9½, DREAMTIME PARTS 1–4)

CHUCK MALY

(DREAMTIME PARTS 5–11)

DARK HORSE BOOKS

President & Publisher MIKE RICHARDSON

Collection Editor SPENCER CUSHING

Collection Assistant Editor KEVIN BURKHALTER

Collection Designer HUNTER SHARP

Digital Art Technician ALLYSON HALLER

Published by Dark Horse Books
A division of Dark Horse Comics, Inc.
10956 SE Main Street
Milwaukie, OR 97222

First edition: November 2016
ISBN 978-1-50670-080-9
1 3 5 7 9 10 8 6 4 2
Printed in China

International Licensing: (503) 905-2377
Comic Shop Locator Service: (888) 266-4226

LIBRARY OF CONGRESS CATALOGING-IN-PUBLICATION DATA

Pini, Wendy.
The Complete ElfQuest Volume Two / by Wendy and Richard Pini. – First edition.
pages cm
Summary: "The Complete ElfQuest Volume 2 Collects ElfQuest: Siege at Blue Mountain and ElfQuest: Kings of the Broken Wheel. This is the second volume in the Complete ElfQuest Series"– Provided by publisher.
ISBN 978-1-61655-408-8 (pbk.)
1. Graphic novels. I. Pini, Richard. II. Title.

PN6728.E45P54 2015
741.5'973–dc23

2014039854

THE COMPLETE ELFQUEST VOLUME 3

This volume collects and reprints the comic books ElfQuest: Hidden Years *#1–#5 and #8–#9½ and the graphic novel* Dreamtime.

TO THOSE WHO DREAM

AND THEN DARE TO SEEK

THE VALIDITY BEHIND THE VISION

CONTENTS

"UH-OH...!"

THIS STORY IS DEDICATED TO MARIA PINI KAPRIELIAN
LASHPAW LOST HIS CHALLENGE! GOLDGRIN IS STILL SECOND CHIEF...
Wolfwood
STORY, SCRIPT AND ART BY WENDY PINI
STORY AND EDITING BY RICHARD PINI

AW, STRONGBOW! YOUR WOLF-FRIEND'S BANISHED! THE PACK'LL NEVER LET HIM NEAR THE HOLT AGAIN.

:SIGH: THAT'S THEIR WAY SOMETIMES.

TOO BAD! YOU AND LASHPAW WERE STUCK TOGETHER LIKE TWO BURRS IN A BOOT!

BONDING TOO CLOSELY WITH A WOLF IS HARD, ISN'T IT, CUTTER?
WE TRY NOT TO, SHENSHEN. BUT SOMETIMES...

BE CAREFUL.

"OUR HEARTS KNOW WHAT THEY WANT, BUT THEY DON'T ALWAYS SEE WELL."

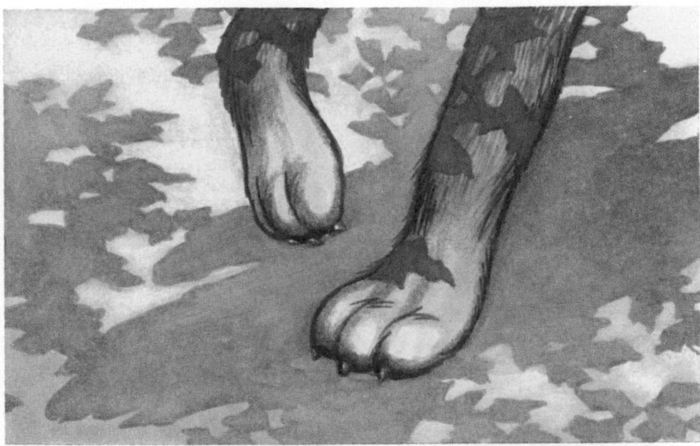

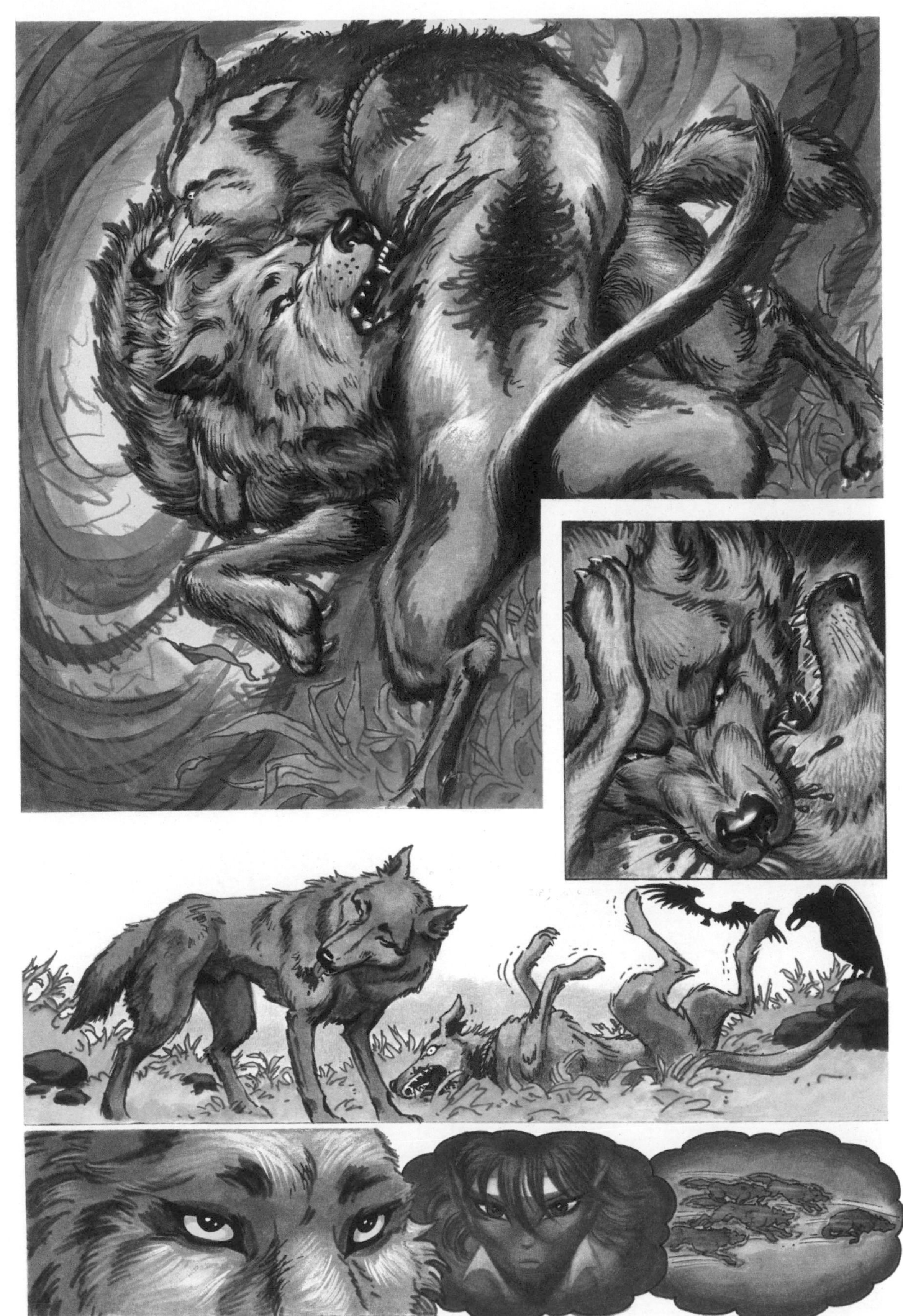

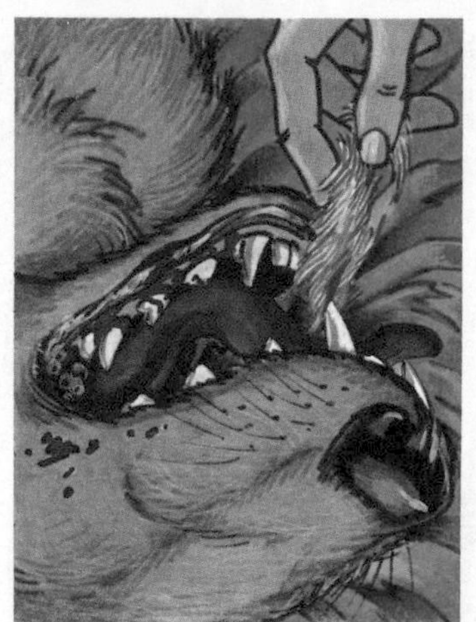

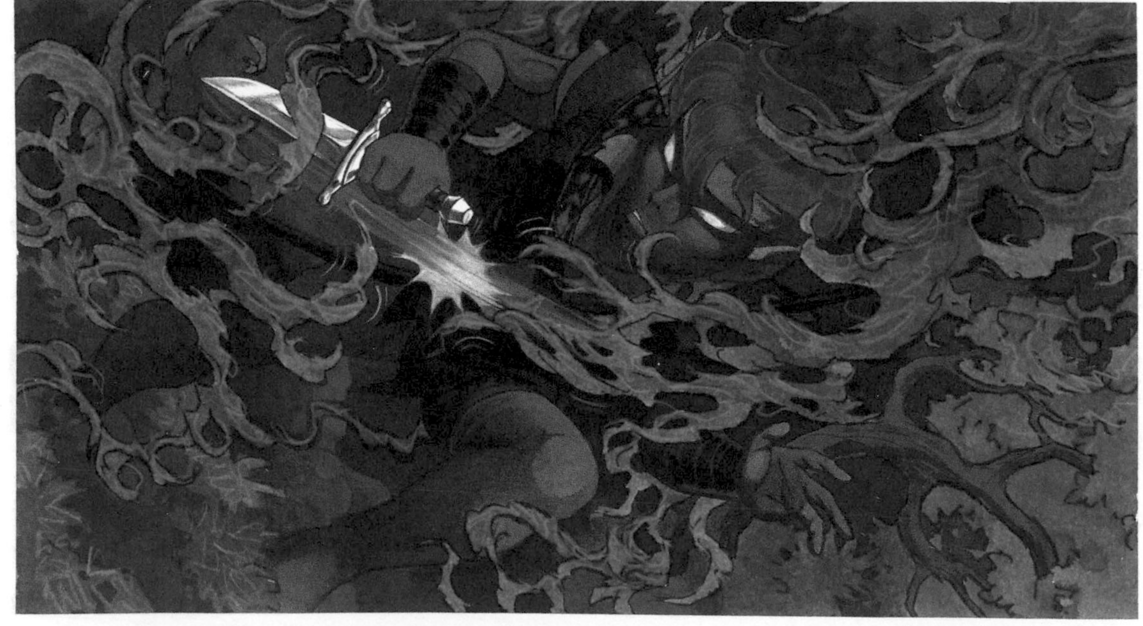

HE'S OUT OF SENDING RANGE NOW.
THAT'S HIS LOOKOUT! IT'S BAD ENOUGH HE TOOK OFF ALONE!

BUT IF ONE OF US... EVEN ONE PRESERVER...GETS CAUGHT TRACKING HIM IN HUMAN TERRITORY...
...OUR SECRET'S OUT! AND THIS HOLT'S FINISHED!

UNLESS WE SENSE DEATH ITSELF ON HIS TRAIL...
...STRONGBOW'S ON HIS OWN!

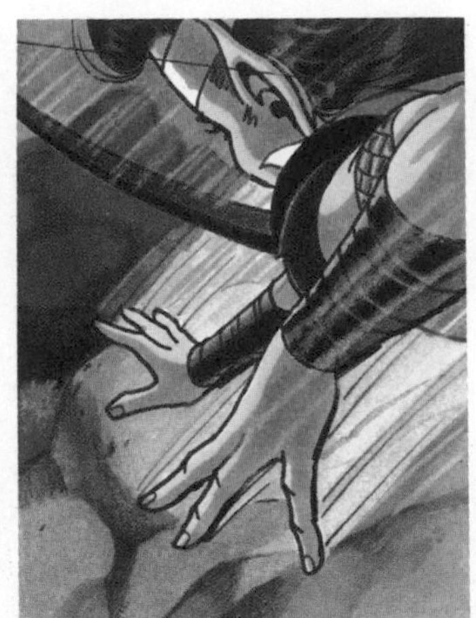

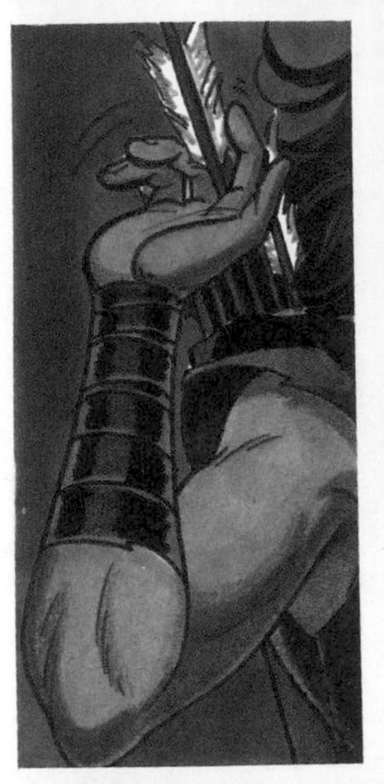

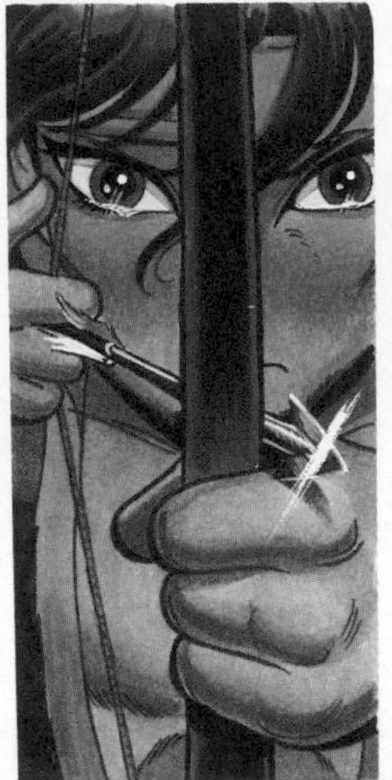

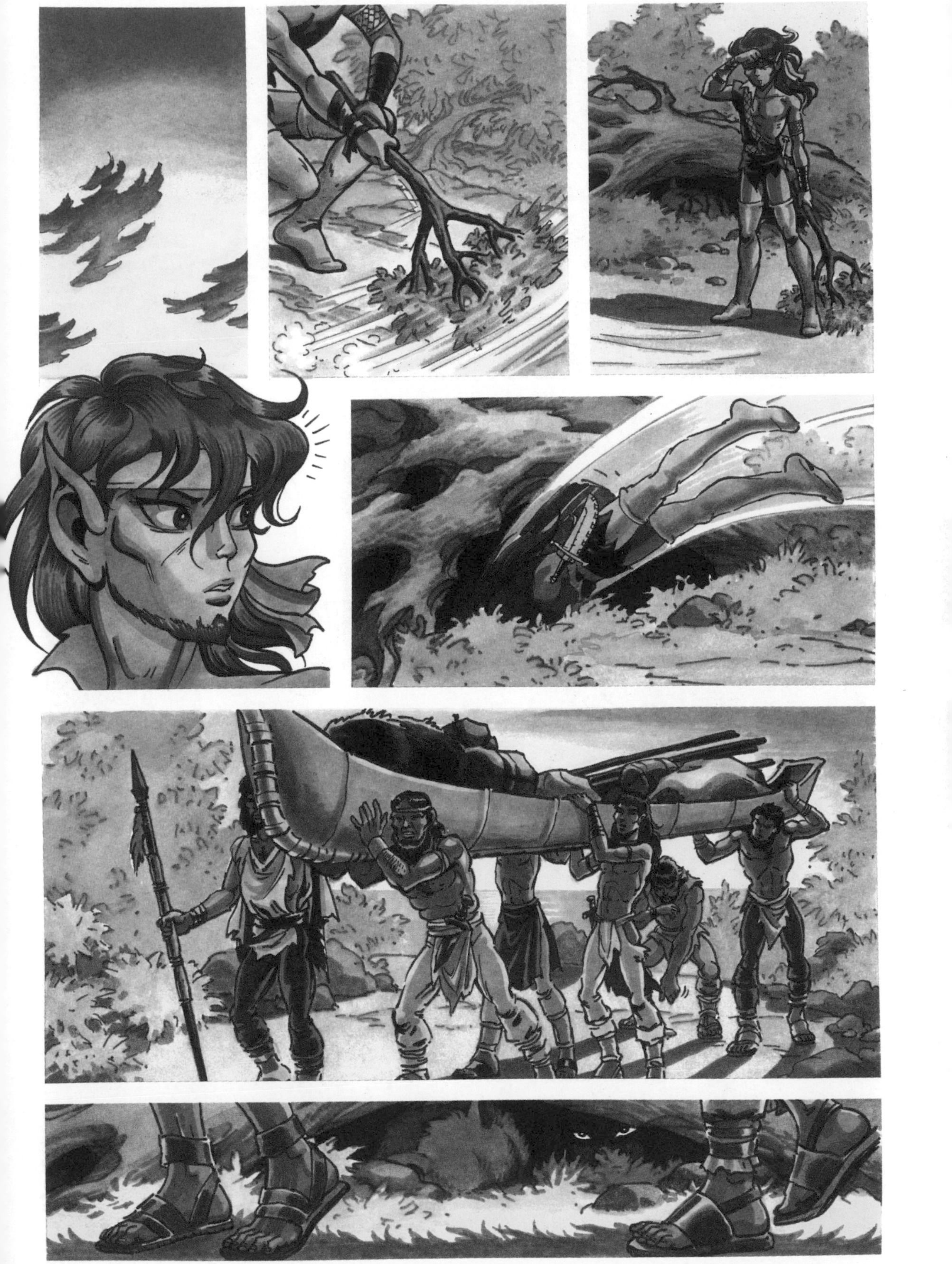

T-TIMMAIN...?

IT IS YOU! CAREFUL... NOT TOO CLOSE!

THUNDER...AND SKYFIRE...INSIDE MY HEAD! SOON... I'LL BE LIKE LASHPAW!
YOU THINK THERE'S HOPE FOR US, HIGH ONE...?
GO ON...I'LL FOLLOW...

GASP
AAGHH!

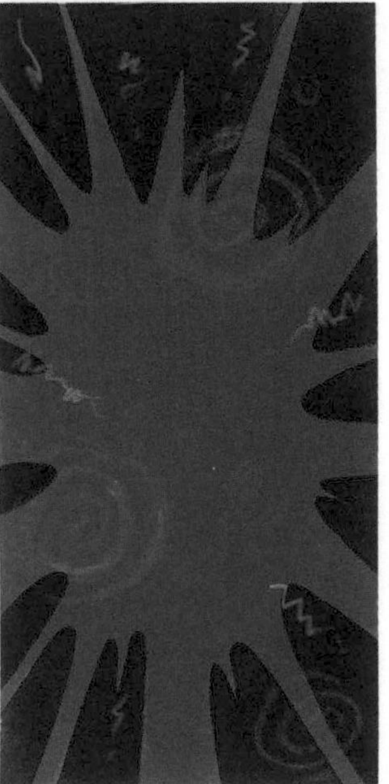

STAY BACK, **MOONSHADE!** THEIR SPIT'S **POISON!**
THE FOAMING SICKNESS! HE WAS COMING TO US FOR HELP!

HE-HE MUST HAVE FORGOTTEN...WE HAVE NO HEALER!
NO...NO HEALER.

WHAT ABOUT THE **TROLLS?!**
OLD MAGGOTY'S BEEN TEASING ME FOR MOONS ABOUT HER MOST SECRET POTIONS!
AND THEY USE **FIRE!** GREAT HEAT CAN CLEANSE GREAT ILLS... SOMETIMES!

GENTLY, LIFEMATE!
WHATEVER PRICE THE TROLLS DEMAND...

"...WE'LL PAY!"

ALL THIS SWEAT, AND THEM BOTH DONE FOR!
IT MAKES NO SENSE!

THIS ISN'T ABOUT SENSE.
ANYTHING FOR FAMILY, EH? GUESS I CAN FAULT YOU ELVES IN ALL WAYS BUT THAT!

HOLD STILL, TWIT! THIS GOES IN, STAYS IN, AND GETS TENDED FOR AS LONG AS IT TAKES!

INTO YOUR BLOOD...INTO YOUR BRAIN...BE CURED OR BE KILLED...HEE HEE HEEEEEEEE...

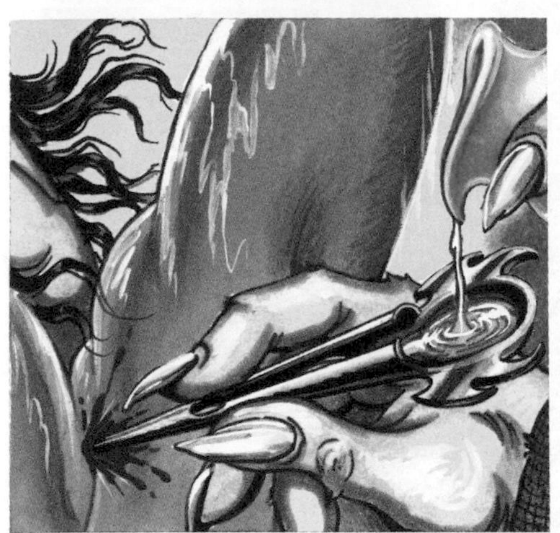

NOW...ONE FOR YOU, STINKING BEAST!
PUH! I'M A FOOL FOR EVEN TRYING THIS!

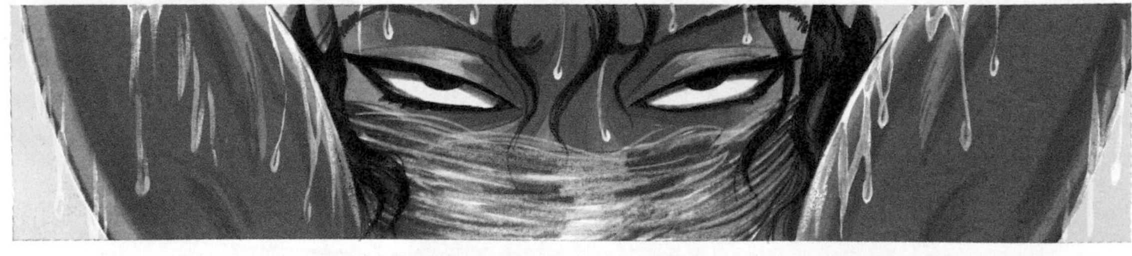

WELL, COAT ME WITH HONEY AND CALL ME BEESWEETS! LASHPAW'S BULLIED HIS WAY BACK IN!
HE'S SECOND CHIEF, NOW! EVER SEE SUCH A STUBBORN FIGHTER?!

YES... THANK THE HIGH ONES!

HEY! NOW, HOW'S THAT FOR SPUNK!

LASHPAW'S EYEING THE CHIEF WOLF NOW!

DON'T GET ANY IDEAS!

Going Back

THERE...! THE HOLE RAYEK DUG TO BAR US GO-BACKS FROM OUR LODGE!

"HOLE"?! WITH THAT MUCH MAGIC IN HIM, NO WONDER HE WAS ABLE TO SPIRIT THE PALACE INTO ANOTHER TIME!

YOU MAY BE CHIEF OF A TRIBE THAT NO LONGER EXISTS, BELOV...EH... KAHVI.

STORY, SCRIPT AND ART BY WENDY PINI
STORY AND EDITING BY RICHARD PINI

BAH! A LITTLE TRENCH LIKE THAT COULDN'T THWART MY WARRIOR FOLK LONG, TYLDAK!
IT'S HONEST BRAGGING I'VE DONE ON THEM ALL THESE CRUSTINGS. WAIT AND SEE!

BUT WE SEND AND SEND...AND NO ANSWER COMES!

TWOINNG

GASP
HIGH ONES!

ROTTEN, POKING TROLL!
!?!

HOLD IT, YOU!

TRY TO MAIM MY BEAUTIFUL BIRD, WILL YOU?! LET'S IMPROVE YOUR FACE...

...BY HALF A NOSE LESS! ...EH?!
WHO ARE YOU, GIRL?
PANT PANT I-I'M JIRDA! WHO ARE YOU?

HA HA HA! LITTLE JIRDA! YOU WEREN'T EVEN UP TO MY BOOT TOP WHEN I LEFT!
I'M KAHVI, YOUR CHIEF!

HEY!
AAARRROOOOOOO

AAARROOOO

...

WELL! SURPRISED LOOKS ON NEW FACES I CAN UNDERSTAND...

"CHIEF" ZEY...?! BORN SINCE I WENT JAUNTING, YES?
WELL! BY ALL MEANS, LEAD ON!

PHWEEET! COME DOWN, BEAUTIFUL BIRD, AND WARM THOSE HOLLOW BONES BY THE FIRE PIT!

BUT...HE-HE'S A MONSTER! HE HAS NO HANDS!
WHAT HE HAS MAKES UP FOR WHAT HE HASN'T, MARDU, BELIEVE ME!

...DON'T ASK ME HOW! RAYEK TOOK THE PALACE TO SOME FAR-AHEAD TIME, THAT'S ALL I KNOW! THERE WAS NO WAY TO GIVE CHASE... NO WAY TO CLAIM REVENGE.
MY DAUGHTER AND I LIVED IN THE NEW LAND WITH THE WOLFRIDERS... WAITING. BUT THE PALACE NEVER CAME BACK.
FINALLY, WHEN VENKA WAS GROWN, TYLDAK AND I SOUGHT THE FROZEN MOUNTAINS TOGETHER. IT TOOK A LONG TIME. THE WOLFRIDER CHIEF WAS RIGHT. I MISSED YOU ALL.

ALL WHO KNEW YOU MANY CRUSTINGS AGO, YOU MEAN!
WE DANCED FOR YOU, ALL RIGHT, SANG YOU PRAISE-FILLED DEATHSONGS.
BUT AS IT TURNS OUT...YOU FAILED! THE PALACE...

...MAY BE GONE FOR GOOD! AYE! MEANTIME, YOU'VE LET YOURSELVES SINK LOWER THAN TROLLS! THAT'S ***YOUR*** FAULT, ***ZEY!***

WHAT HAPPENED TO ***URDA?*** I LEFT HER IN CHARGE!

TROLLS AMBUSHED HER HUNTING PARTY...TOOK THEM ALL UNDERGROUND. WE GOT EVEN.

THAT'S HOW IT'S BEEN. AND THAT'S ALL THERE IS. WHAT DID YOU EXPECT?

WE'RE GO-BACKS WITH NOTHING TO GO BACK TO...EVER... FROM WHAT YOU SAY.

OH...?

AND HOW WOULD IT BE IF I TOLD YOU I KNOW WHERE TO LAY HANDS ON A ***PIECE*** OF THE PALACE...

THE ONLY PIECE LEFT IN THE WORLD?

...!

WHERE...? WH-WHERE...
NEVER YOU MIND! GIVE ME PROVISIONS, A COUPLE OF SHARP HUNTERS, AND FIGHTING STAGS FIT FOR A ROUGH TREK.
WE'LL BE BACK BEFORE THE NEW GREEN FADES.

FAIR ENOUGH?

A QUEST! A REAL QUEST! COUNT ME IN!
AND ME... OUT! LEAVE THE FROZEN MOUNTAINS? NOT EVEN FOR A PIECE OF THE PALACE!

"BETTER TO STAY HERE AND DEAL WITH THE ENEMIES WE KNOW!"

DON'T TRY TO SEND, CHOT. I KNOW IT'S A STRAIN.
JUST TAKE THIS IN...

I DON'T THINK KAHVI IS LYING.
I THINK SHE MAY EVEN SUCCEED. THAT WILL MAKE HER A HERO.

AND WHAT WILL THAT MAKE ME...
...OR YOU, MY FRIEND?

DISAPPOINTED?
THEY'VE LOST SOMETHING... PRIDE, GUTS, HEART MAYBE...I DON'T KNOW. THEY NEED RAISING UP.
THEY NEED THE PALACE.

IT'S YOU THEY NEED... AS DO I.
FOOLISH BIRD! NOTHING'S SPECIAL ABOUT ME! ALL I CAN DO IS FETCH THE GO-BACKS THE LAST SCRAP OF WHAT THEY LIVED... AND DIED FOR! IT'S THEIR RIGHT!
AND I CAN ONLY STAND BY YOU...

"...DEFEND YOU... EVEN FROM YOURSELF."
WELL, CHOT... YUN...YOU WERE RUNNY-NOSED AND BARE-RUMPED LAST TIME I SAW YOU!
LET'S SEE WHAT YOU'RE MADE OF NOW!
DAYS LATER, FAR AHEAD OF HIS MUCH SLOWER TRAVELING COMPANIONS, TYLDAK CIRCLES ABOVE THE GIGANTIC, BAROQUE BURIAL MOUND WHICH WAS ONCE HIS HOME...BLUE MOUNTAIN.

REEVOL'S BOND BIRD, FROM THE LOOK OF THE HARNESS...THOUGH THERE'S LITTLE ENOUGH LEFT BY WHICH TO JUDGE.
THE BODIES OF MY PEOPLE WERE CRUSHED BENEATH THESE ROCKS. THEIR SPIRITS FLEW TO THE PALACE OF THE HIGH ONES.
WHAT PART OF THEM REMAINS WITHIN THE TINY RELIC WE SEEK, I WONDER...?

SKAAAAAWWW!
SKAAAAWW!

KUREEL'S SECOND FLEDGELING...MANY YEARS GROWN! AND WITH YOUNG, BY THEIR MARKINGS...

YES, YOU REMEMBER ME! YOU'VE KEPT AS CLOSE TO YOUR OLD AERIES AS YOU COULD!
BRED TO SERVE! LET'S HOPE YOU'VE PASSED THE GLIDERS' TRAINING ON TO YOUR CHICKS!

ELSEWHERE...
I HARDLY REMEMBER RAYEK...
BUT HE LEFT WISPS OF TALES THAT ALWAYS MADE ME WONDER.
ARE YOU SURE THE SUN FOLK WILL FIGHT, KAHVI?
WOULDN'T YOU? THEY'RE NOT THE SOFTLINGS THEY USED TO BE. THE VILLAGE IS SEEDED WITH WOLFRIDERS!

WE'LL TRY STEALTH FIRST AND, FAILING THAT, WE'LL SCARE 'EM GOOD!
IF THEY'RE SMART THEY'LL GIVE UP BEFORE ANY BLOOD IS SHED.
I HOPE SO!

BUT THERE MAY BE AN EVEN BIGGER FIGHT WHEN WE RETURN TO THE LODGE! ZEY LIKES BEING CHIEF...VERY, VERY MUCH AND...
LOOK!

THREE GREAT HAWKS! TYLDAK'S BROUGHT THEM JUST AS YOU SAID HE WOULD, KAHVI!

AH, CHOT! MY WINGED FRIEND WOULD BRING ME BOTH MOONS IF I CHARGED HIM TO!

WE'LL BE A WHILE LEARNING TO STEER THOSE OVERFED SHRIEK-OWLS...

"...BUT THE SUN FOLK AREN'T GOING ANYWHERE! THEY'RE ROOTED DEEP AS THE RABBIT FODDER THEY GROW IN THEIR GARDENS!"

♫ SEE! THE TIME OF FLOOD AND FLOWER! DESERT GOWNED IN COLORS BRIGHT! ♪

RAINBOW VEILED, HER SKY-BLUE BROW! HER ♫ BLOSSOMS SWEETLY SCENT THE NIGHT!

WING... BELOVED...?
OF COURSE, BEHTIA! SOON, CARRYING THINGS WILL BE MUCH EASIER FOR YOU!
VERY SOON, I'D SAY!

PERHAPS... TOMORROW!
I FEEL IT TOO, MENDER!
YIPE!

A BEE...!
...MISTOOK YOU FOR A BLOOM, SWEET LIFEMATE!
THAT'S EASILY FIXED!

WHA...?! OH! :GIGGLE: WINDKIN!
FOLLOW ME TO YOUR PLACE OF HONOR, BEHTIA! YOU STAND FOR ALL WE CELEBRATE!
RECOGNITION AT FESTIVAL! SAME TIME, TWO YEARS LATER, A CUB! THAT HASN'T HAPPENED SINCE...SINCE WHO KNOWS?

POF
POF
POF

SAVAH, THE MOTHER OF MEMORY, HAS LIT THE LANTERNS! THE NEW GREEN'S SPROUTED, THE HARVEST FOLLOWS!
SING AND DANCE FOR JOY!
HA HA HA! SOON AS YOU MOVE OFF THE MAT, TRY AND STOP US, DART!

AS THE NIGHT REELS ONWARD AND THE STARS BEGIN TO FADE, THE REVELRY GROWS, IF ANYTHING, EVEN MORE BOISTEROUS.

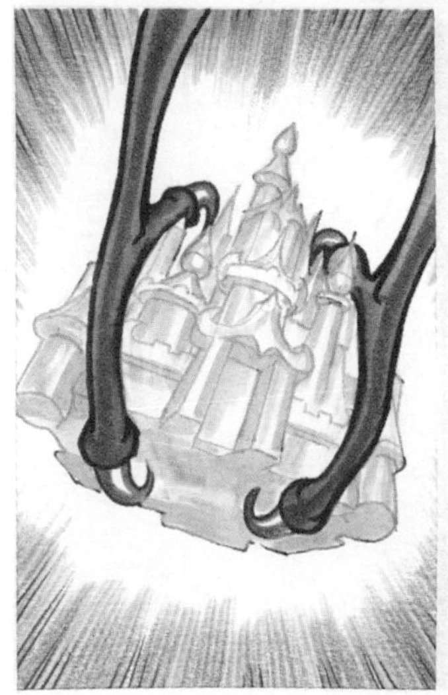

FORTUNATELY, THOUGH DAZED BY DREAMBERRY JUICE, SCOUTER CHOOSES THAT MOMENT TO LOOK UP...

...AND A FRENZY OF A DIFFERENT SORT SEIZES THE VILLAGERS.
WHO... WHAT IS IT?!
STOP!
NO, DART! WOUND HIM AND HE MAY DROP THE LITTLE PALACE!
TYLDAK! I THOUGHT WE WERE DONE WITH HIM!

!?!

YOU! I FORGOT!

SO YOU'RE MY SIRE.
I'VE TRIED TO THINK WELL OF YOU...'TIL NOW.

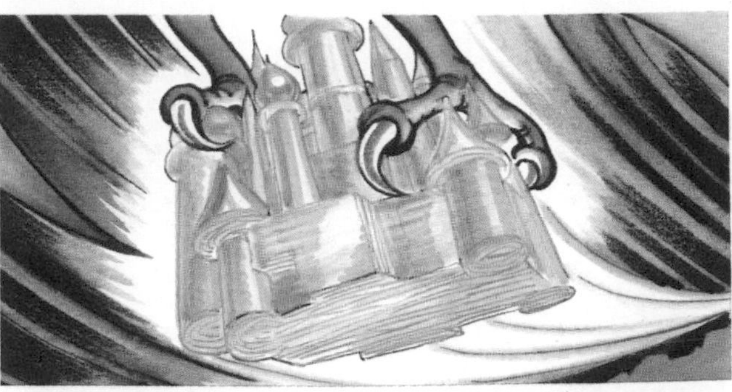

HE IS AS I WAS BEFORE I RECEIVED MY WINGS...
...LACKING SPEED, OR HEIGHT. YET, LOOK HOW FIERCELY HE PURSUES!
WAIT!

FLYHIGHTHING FAST! WE FASTER! PTHOOO!
SPOOT!
GUPTH!

GASP
GAG COUGH COUGH

WHEW!

RREEAAAAWWK!
RRAAWWK! RRAAAWWK!

PANT PANT AHDRI! HIDE THIS... PANT ...SAVAH'S HUT! DOWNSTAIRS!
GOOD IDEA!

EVERYONE! TO YOUR UNDERGROUND ROOMS!

WHY... WHY, IT IS KAHVI!
SHE WON'T HARM YOU WHILE I LIVE! HURRY, SAVAH!
GO ON! RUN! RUN! DOWN INTO YOUR ROOT HOLES!
THINK THAT'LL SAVE YOU?! HA HA HA!

THEY CALL THESE LODGES?! WE CAN RIP THE LIDS RIGHT OFF THESE CLAY POTS, EASY!
TOO BAD! I HOPE THE SUN FOLK SURRENDER QUICKLY!
HEAR ME, DESERT DWELLERS!
WE WANT BUT ONE THING, AND THAT YOU KNOW!
HAND IT OVER AND WE GO IN PEACE! REFUSE, AND IT'S YOUR GARDENS... THEN...

"...YOUR WELL!"
DO NOT FEAR FOR ME, WING! I AM ONE JAR THAT WILL NOT LOSE ITS LID UNTIL IT IS TIME!
SHE'S WEAKENING THE ROOF WITH BOULDERS! BUT SHE'LL HAVE TO DISMOUNT TO GET AT US! THEN IT'S HAND TO HAND!
SELF-BLAME, CHILD? WHY IN THE WORLD...?
SCOUTER IS MY FATHER, BUT TYLDAK'S MY BLOOD!
AND HE'S HELPING TO DESTROY OUR HOME! OUR BEAUTIFUL HOME...!
I-I CAN'T LET...
WHOA! THE UPPER DOME'S FALLEN THROUGH!
NO!
WINDKIN! DON'T... OOWWW!

HMH! THE LAD SEEKS TO LURE US AWAY FROM THE VILLAGE!
TAKE HIM UP ON IT, BEAUTIFUL BIRD! THESE HAWKS AREN'T MADE FOR DELICATE MANEUVERS!

EVEN THAT BIT OF PALACE HAS THE POWER TO INCREASE HIS SPEED!

BUT NOT ENOUGH!

HUH?!

HERE! IT IS YOURS!
SIGH THAT'S IT, THEN! CHOT! YUN! LET'S GO!
ARROGANT! SHE RIDES WITH-OUT A HALTER LOOP!

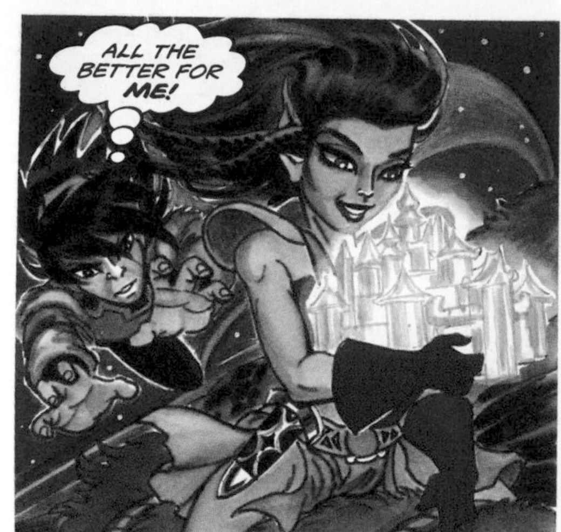
ALL THE BETTER FOR ME!

?!!

KAHVI!

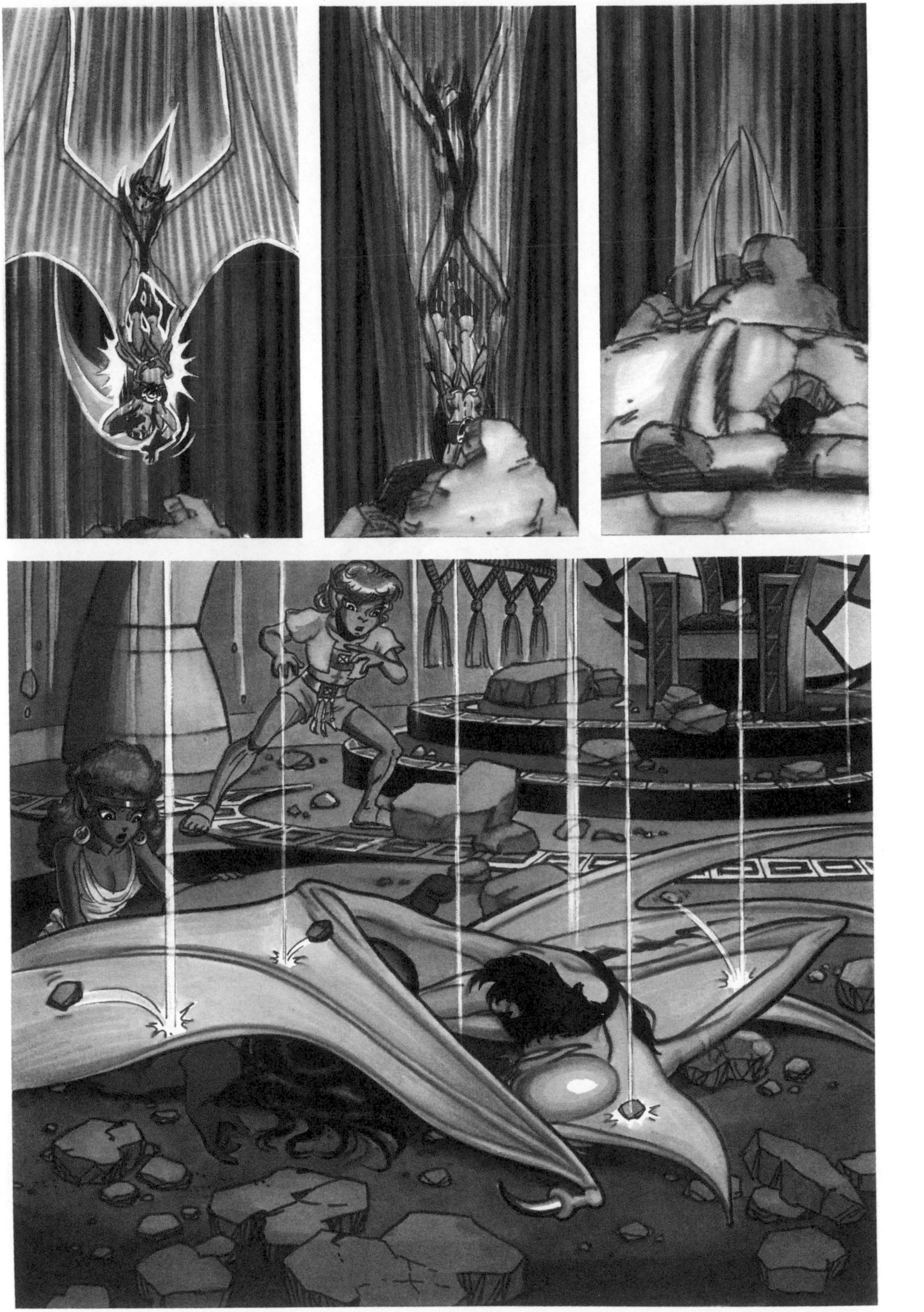

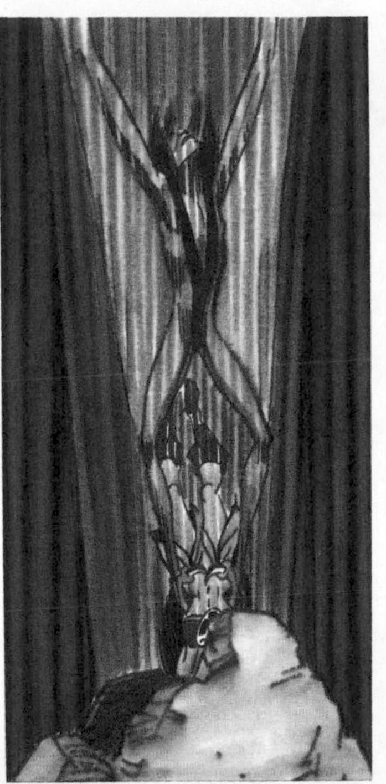

HELLO!
HELLO NICE FLYHIGHTHING!
≈PANT PANT PANT≈ WHERE *WERE* YOU THREE?! LOOK! THEY'VE GOT THE LITTLE PALACE!

≈GASP GASP≈ I'M THROUGH! AFTER THEM, PRESERVERS! *FLY!*

HURRY! HURRY!
NASTYBAD HIGHTHINGS!

ZEY AND YOU... PLANNED THIS, *CHOT?* IT *STINKS!* WE CAN'T LEAVE *KAHVI* AND *TYLDAK* BACK THERE!
THE PALACE... WAIT 'TIL YOU HOLD IT IN YOUR ARMS! THERE'S NO FEELING LIKE IT!

ON THE OTHER HAND...I THINK I'LL KEEP IT TO MYSELF!
THE ONE WHO BRINGS IT TO THE GO-BACKS... ONLY *HE* DESERVES TO BE CHIEF!

HIGHTHING DO RIGHT THING!

HIGHTHING DO RIGHT THING!

HIGHTHING DO RIGHT THING!

HERE! TAKE IT! I'M LOYAL TO KAHVI! MAKE THEM LET HER GO!
IT ISN'T THAT EASY!

KAHVI... TYLDAK...WE ARE RELIEVED THAT, THANKS TO MENDER, YOU SURVIVED YOUR FALL.
BUT WHAT ARE YOU TO DO WITH US NOW, EH... NOW THAT THE LITTLE PALACE IS YOURS AGAIN?
YOU DAREN'T RELEASE US! IN THE GO-BACKS' NAME, WE'LL KEEP FIGHTING TO RECLAIM WHAT'S OURS!
ONE WAY OR ANOTHER WE'LL MAKE THINGS VERY MESSY FOR YOU!

IT HAS EVER BEEN MY BELIEF THAT ALL ELVES, EVEN WARRIORS, WANT PEACE ABOVE ALL. WE CANNOT GIVE YOU THE RELIC...
...BUT WE CAN INVITE THE GO-BACKS TO DWELL HERE, AS SOME OF THE WOLFRIDERS DO. WE HAVE THE ROOM, AND THE LOVE.

PTOO!

KAHVI... YOUR OWN TRIBESMAN BETRAYED YOU.
PERHAPS IT'S WISEST, AFTER ALL, TO FORGET THE GO-BACKS. THEY'RE NOT WORTH...

...IT'S WORTH MY LIFE TO RAISE THEM UP TO WHAT THEY WERE! UNDERSTAND?
HOWEVER THEY SEE ME NOW, I WAS THEIR CHIEF. AND THEY'RE MY PEOPLE!

GIVE US HALF, THEN!

HALF?! HERE! TAKE HALF MY HEAD OR HALF MY CHEST!

THE LITTLE PALACE HELPS US KEEP TRACK OF OUR BLOOD KIN ACROSS THE SEA...YOU **KNOW** THAT! BREAK IT IN TWO OVER MY COLD CARCASS!
SO WE **BOTH** HAVE SOMETHING TO DIE FOR! BEST YOU FINISH ME, THEN, WOLFRIDER!

FINISH ME NOW...!
UNGH!
OOF!
...OR I'LL MAKE YOU WISH YOU HAD!

YOU'VE NEVER LET ME LOVE YOU AS I'D LIKE.
I SWORE TO DEFEND YOU...FROM YOU...IF NEED BE.

TIME TO REST...TIME TO DREAM A DIFFERENT DREAM...

...BELOVED!
CURSE YOU! CURSE YOUR HOLLOW BONES...

SAVAH...THIS IS YUN. SHE COULD HAVE FLED, BUT SHE BROUGHT THE LITTLE PALACE BACK TO US!
AS WINDKIN FAVORS HIS MOTHER IN SIZE AND SPIRIT...
SO, I THINK, YOU FAVOR YOUR FATHER, YUN.

H-HOW LONG...WILL KAHVI AND TYLDAK...?
WHO KNOWS? BUT WHAT BETTER WAY FOR THEM TO COOL OFF?

IF IT'S ALL RIGHT... I THINK I'LL WAIT HERE FOR THEM. I'VE NEVER SEEN THE DESERT BEFORE, OR SUCH STRANGE LODGES...
...OR EVEN STARS AS BRIGHT AS YOURS...

Little Patch
THIS STORY IS DEDICATED TO TROY PICCONE
BACK FROM THEIR JOURNEY THROUGH TIME, SKYWISE, LEETAH, AND THE TWINS LEARN HOW THE PASSING YEARS HAVE AFFECTED THEIR ADOPTED LAND, THEIR HOLT, AND THEIR TRIBE...
CHOPLICKER DOESN'T KNOW ANY OF THE WOLFRIDERS' NEW WOLVES. HOW WILL HE FIT INTO THE PACK?
HE'LL FIND A WAY, EMBER.

ANYHOW, HE NEED FEAR NO CHALLENGE FROM ***PATIENCE.*** SHE'S A BIT DULL AS WOLVES GO. I'M OFTEN TEASED ABOUT IT.

WHO WOULDN'T FEEL PEACEFUL NEAR YOU, ***TYLEET?*** YOU'RE SO CALM AND GENTLE...

WELL, THANKS TO LEETAH, I HAD A WONDERFUL START!
HEH HEH...NEVER KNOWING A MOMENT'S WANT, TRULY, I'M SPOILED BEYOND HOPE!

WHEN YOU...CUTTER'S FAMILY...DISAPPEARED, YOU LEFT A GREAT EMPTINESS BEHIND. IN PART, I GUESS I FILLED IT.
WHAT CAN IT HAVE BEEN LIKE... FOR HIM?
WHO KNOWS...?

"WHO CAN EVER *REALLY* KNOW? BUT BECAUSE CUTTER NEVER FORGOT YOU, *WE* NEVER FORGOT.

"SO EVEN THOUGH YOU WERE LOST IN A FAR-AHEAD TIME, YOU WERE ALL STILL PART OF US."

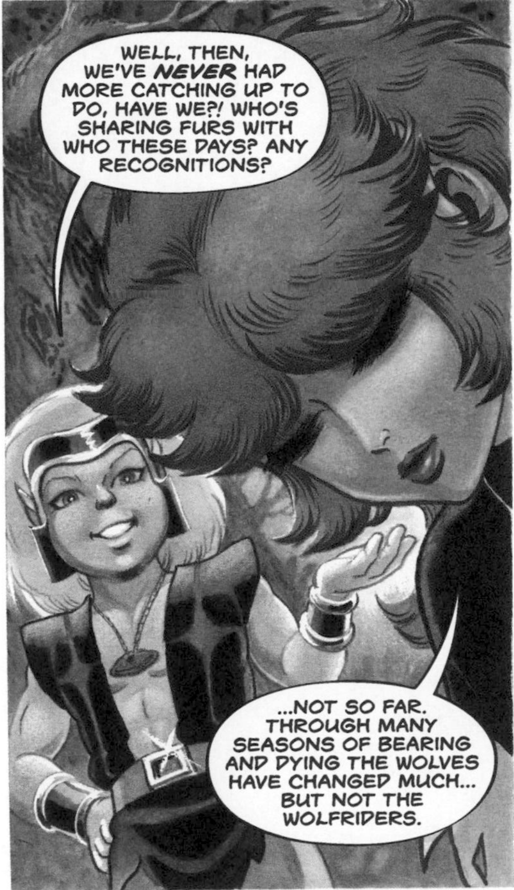

WELL, THEN, WE'VE *NEVER* HAD MORE CATCHING UP TO DO, HAVE WE?! WHO'S SHARING FURS WITH WHO THESE DAYS? ANY RECOGNITIONS?
...NOT SO FAR. THROUGH MANY SEASONS OF BEARING AND DYING THE WOLVES HAVE CHANGED MUCH... BUT NOT THE WOLFRIDERS.

IT'S FOR THE BEST, SINCE THE HUMANS HERE BREED LIKE FLEAS!
WE WERE USED TO THEM MOSTLY AS SMALL, WANDERING TRIBES. NOW THEY STAY VERY PUT AND SPREAD OUT FROM THERE!

BUT EVEN THOUGH I'VE NEVER BEEN RECOGNIZED...I **DID** HAVE A CUB ONCE.
A CUB?! WITHOUT A HEALER'S AID?! HOW...?

BETWEEN THEN AND NOW, I SPENT MORE TIME ASLEEP THAN MY MIND CAN GRASP.
BUT MY HEART KNOWS IT WASN'T SO LONG AGO...

HERE...LOCK-SEND AND I'LL SHARE WITH YOU.

IT HAPPENS IN THE SEASON OF DEATH-SLEEP...

A SMALL, COLD RAIN HELPS THE CAPNUTS DROP 'TIL THEY COVER THE GROUND.

CAPNUTS... MY FAVORITE.

THOUGH IT'S DAYLIGHT, I'M NOT SLEEPY. THE GRAY MIST SAFELY CLOAKS ME WHILE I GO GATHERING.

THEN...FAR FROM THE HOLT, I HEAR...

?!?

IS IT A FOX SQUEALING IN A HUMAN SNARE? I FOLLOW THOSE ODD, BROKEN WAILS, MAKING MANY GUESSES...

...ALL OF THEM WRONG!

A HUMAN CUB, FRESH BORN, LIFE CORD STILL THROBBING AND UNEATEN!

"THIS IS A MISTAKE, OF COURSE," I TELL ME. "SUCH A STRONG, HEALTHY CUB!"
SO I BACKTRACK A SCENT TRAIL...

...DOWN PAST FATHER'S THORN WALL... PAST WHERE THE TREE TRUNKS NARROW AND MUCH WOOD HAS BEEN CUT...TO AN OPEN PLACE WHERE A HUMAN TRIBE LIVES, SURROUNDED BY ITS OWN WALL OF PILED STONES.

WHEN THEIR FIRES DIE AND EVEN THEIR SCOUTS SAG WITH SLEEP...

...I SQUEEZE BETWEEN THE SPIKES...
...MATCH SCENT WITH SCENT, FIX THE HUNGRY CUB TO THE THATCH, AND FLEE...

...JUST IN TIME!

GOOD! NOW HIS MOTHER'S WARM BREAST WILL COMFORT HIM.

BUT AS DAWN GLIMMERS THROUGH THE LEAVES...

!?!

WAAAAHHH AA-HUH! AA-HUH! AAAAAAAAAA!

SEEING, I CAN'T BELIEVE, MUCH LESS UNDERSTAND! THE HUMAN MOTHER WEEPS, BUT SEEMS SET ON PINNING HER CUB TO THE TREE!

THE BLOW THEY CAN'T, FINALLY, BEAR TO STRIKE MIGHT HAVE BEEN A MERCY. THE POOR CUB IS NEARLY DEAD FROM MISUSE.
SOME THINGS YOU JUST CAN'T LET BE.

AM I CONCERNED THAT THE OTHERS MIGHT OBJECT?
WELL, PIKE HAS MADE UP A SONG ABOUT ME. IT GOES, "TRY...

"...JUST TRY TO REFUSE HER ANYTHING!"

FEEDING IS NO PROBLEM...
...BUT I MISS HOLDING THE CUB IN MY ARMS.

SO MOTHER RUBS MY BACK 'TIL MY OWN MILK COMES IN.

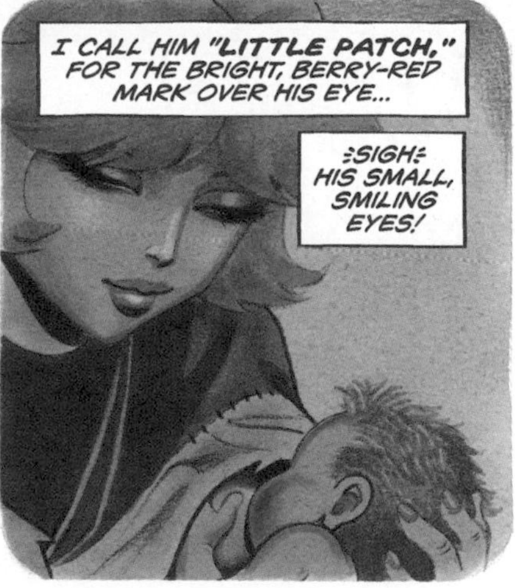
I CALL HIM "LITTLE PATCH," FOR THE BRIGHT, BERRY-RED MARK OVER HIS EYE...
:SIGH: HIS SMALL, SMILING EYES!

DO THE OTHERS LOVE HIM? NO MORE OR LESS, I SUPPOSE, THAN THEY WOULD A STRAY BEAR CUB...

WHICH IS WHY, AS HIS TEETH COME IN AND HE BEGINS TO WALK AND TALK, WORRIES RISE ABOUT THE DANGERS HE MIGHT POSE TO THE TRIBE.

HE'S NOISIER THAN AN ELF CHILD..

IT COMES TO THIS: FIT IN OR BE BANISHED! BUT EVERYONE KNOWS PIKE'S SONG, SO EVERYONE KNOWS THERE'S SIMPLY NO "OR" ABOUT IT! MY SON MUST BECOME A WOLFRIDER!

FATHER AND MOTHER ARE GENEROUS WITH THEIR TEACHINGS OF WOODLORE AND THE MANY USES OF BLADES.

AND THOUGH HAVING TO TALK MAKES STRONGBOW GROWL AT FIRST, HE SOON SEES THAT HUMANS CAN LEARN QUICKLY AND AIM TRUE.

BY THE COMING OF HIS FOURTH NEW-GREEN EVEN LITTLE PATCH'S SCENT IS LIKE OURS!

FROM WATCHING **CUTTER** WHO, I'M TOLD, ONCE FEARED HEIGHTS-- THINK OF IT! HEIGHTS!--MY SON LEARNS TO FLY FROM BRANCH TO BRANCH LIKE A BIRD.

THE TRIBE COMES TO ENJOY THE LESSONS, DIGGING UP EVEN THE MOST ANCIENT OF WOLF LORE...

...LIKE WHERE AND HOW TO CACHE A KILL.
HMPH! WRAPSTUFF BETTER!

AS FOR **WRESTLING**...
...I SUSPECT **PIKE**, **SKOT**, AND **KRIM** TEASE MORE THAN TEACH!

CLEARBROOK AND VENKA GET HIM, MOST TIMES, TO THINK BEFORE ACTING.

WHILE MOONSHADE SHOWS HIM THE SECRET OF SILENCE AND THE MANY WAYS OF HIDING IN PLAIN SIGHT.

ZHANTEE AND SHENSHEN REVIVE SKILL-GAMES FROM THE SUN VILLAGE.

WE ALL LEARN FROM THOSE! SOMETIMES PAINFULLY!

LITTLE PATCH OBEYS OUR RULES AND HIDES FROM THE TALL ONES EVEN AS WE DO. BECAUSE HE CAN'T SEND, WE TEACH HIM SECRET HOWLS AND BIRDCALLS.
THE SHRILL WHISTLE MEANING "STOP! DANGER!" SAVES HIS LIFE...MORE THAN ONCE!

I'M PROUD OF HIM...AND OF ME, FOR BEING PROVED RIGHT! SEE HOW MY SON HOLDS HIS OWN AS A WOLFRIDER! HE'S FLEET AND CLEVER. AND, IN HIS WAY, BEAUTIFUL.

"TALL ONE"...! I'M AFRAID I IGNORE WHAT THAT MEANS UNTIL, OVERNIGHT IT SEEMS, HE SHOOTS UP LIKE A MOONWEED!

IT'S A SURPRISE TO HIM TOO. HE BECOMES AWKWARD, MISJUDGING BOTH THE LENGTH OF HIS OWN LIMBS...

...AND THEIR GROWING STRENGTH.
HE FEELS A NEW WARINESS IN SOME OF US. IT HURTS...

...AS DO THE STRANGE STIRRINGS WITHIN HIM.

HOW TO HONOR THOSE STIRRINGS? IT TAKES AT LEAST TWO...JOINED, AT THE VERY LEAST, IN DESIRE. BUT IN US THERE IS NO ANSWERING URGE.

IT SO HAPPENS AROREE WAS ONCE "CURIOUS" WITH THE KEPT HUMANS OF BLUE MOUNTAIN.

BUT, IN ALL INTENDED GENTLENESS, SHE'S FORGOTTEN...OUR BLOODSONG IS PITCHED MUCH HIGHER THAN THEY CAN BEAR.
IT GOES BADLY.

CLOSE...NEVER TO BE CLOSER. ONE OF US... BUT NOT.
MY SON RUNS AWAY...
...SEEKING HIS OWN KIND, FULLY MINDFUL OF CUTTER'S STRICTEST RULE...

"...SHOULD HE EVER CHOOSE TO REJOIN HIS HUMAN TRIBE, **LITTLE PATCH,** ON PAIN OF DEATH, MUST **NEVER** RETURN TO THE HOLT!
MUTE, FULL OF LONGING... HE OFFERS HIMSELF. WATCHING FROM THE TREES, I THINK...
WHO WOULD **NOT** WANT HIM?!
AND YET...

WHY? WHY HIS ABANDONMENT AT BIRTH? WHY THIS REJECTION NOW?
POOR CUB...CAUGHT BETWEEN A WORLD HE CAN NO LONGER HAVE AND ONE THAT WON'T HAVE HIM!

HE'S READY TO GIVE UP. IT'S A CHOICE I CAN'T HONOR.

THE "STOP! DANGER!" WHISTLE PUTS AN END TO THAT NONSENSE! I WATCH HIM RECONSIDER...

...AND TRY A DIFFERENT PATH.

HIS BOLDNESS CATCHES THEM BY SURPRISE. BEFORE DRIVING HIM AWAY AGAIN, THEY ACCEPT HIS GIFT...
...AND OFFER ONE IN RETURN...

...AN EXPLANATION!

WOLVES, OF COURSE, WILL SWIFTLY RID THEMSELVES OF THE SICK OR UNSOUND AMONG THEM.

WHY MY CUB'S MARKINGS MAKE HIM SEEM UNFIT TO HIS HUMAN PACK I'LL NEVER KNOW.

BUT AT LEAST HE'S LEARNED THE TROUBLE IS IN THEM, NOT IN HIM. THE POWER IS NOW HIS TO TREAD GENTLY... CALM THEIR FEARS LITTLE BY LITTLE...

...GAIN THEIR TRUST...

...THROUGH LAUGHTER AND A MASK OF BERRY STAIN SAYING, WITHOUT WORDS, "I MEAN NO HARM."

IT WILL TAKE TIME.

I'VE HEARD THAT HUMANS BELIEVE ANGRY SPIRITS BECOME FLESH AGAIN TO TAKE REVENGE. MANY DAYS PASS BEFORE **PATCH** IS ALLOWED INSIDE THE WALL.

AND STILL HE IS SHUNNED, ESPECIALLY BY THOSE WHO BORE HIM.

THOUGH BARRED FROM THEIR DENS, HE'S FINALLY PERMITTED HIS OWN FIRE.
...A GREAT DAY!

SIMPLY, HE OUT-HUNTS, OUT-PROTECTS, OUT-PROVIDES, AND OUT-GRACES ANYONE IN THE CAMP.

LEARNING THEIR TONGUE, HE WINS THEM WITH HIS CAREFUL CHOICE OF WORDS AS WELL AS HIS DEEDS.

BECAUSE HE HARDLY SPEAKS OF HIMSELF... AND NEVER OF US... HE'S AN ENTICING MYSTERY!

BUT THERE IS ONE, CONTENT WITH HIS SECRETS, WHO SEES-- AND PREFERS--WHAT LIES BENEATH THE MASK.

HUNGRY CUB...DOES HE SHUDDER IN THE NOW? OR AT THE MEMORY OF A SEARING FOUR-FINGERED TOUCH?
WHATEVER HE FINDS, IT'S ENOUGH FOR HIM.

BUT TALL ONES DON'T HAVE RECOGNITION. THEY REQUIRE CEREMONIES AND VOWS.
BEFORE LIFEMATING THERE MUST COME TESTS...OF RIGHT TO OWNERSHIP!

THEY TELL **PATCH** WHAT HE MUST DO TO BECOME ONE OF THEM FOR LIFE.

"I HAVE TO WONDER... DOES HE THINK OF US--OF ME--AND ALL WE TAUGHT HIM OF SELF-LOVE, SELF-HONOR?

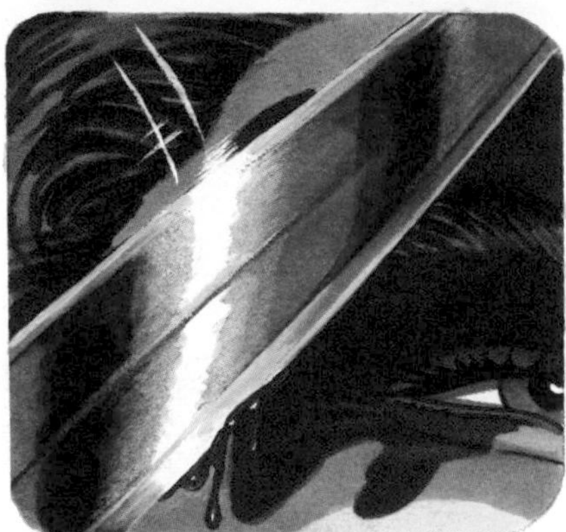

PERHAPS HE DOES...AND STILL CHOOSES TO BE FULLY HUMAN, PAIN AND ALL.

HIS NEW TRIBE VALUES THE SHOWING OF ENDURANCE ABOVE THE SHOWING OF LOVE.
HE'S PROVED HIS WILLINGNESS TO DO THINGS **THEIR** WAY!

MY CUB...

...MY **LITTLE PATCH**...

HE NEVER BETRAYS US...ALWAYS MAKES SURE TO GUIDE HUNTING PARTIES AWAY FROM OUR TERRITORY.

HIS TRIBEMATES DON'T KNOW I WATCH OVER HIM, OR THAT CERTAIN CALLS AND HOWLS ARE MEANT FOR HIM ALONE.

CUTTER SCOLDS ME FOR TAKING SUCH RISKS. BUT WHO BETTER THAN HE KNOWS WHAT IT IS TO ACHE AFTER LOST CUBS?

FOR ME, THE ACHE GOES AWAY, IN TIME.

AND, IN TIME, SOMETHING DRAWS ME BACK TO THE OPEN PLACE...
...WHERE THE TALL ONES ARE MENDING THEIR WALL OF STONES.

HIS STANCE... STILL MORE GRACEFUL THAN ANY OTHER HUMAN'S...HIS COLORING...THE PUCKERED SCAR AT HIS TEMPLE...! I REMEMBER!
LITTLE PATCH HAS BECOME THEIR CHIEF! HE'S BROUGHT THEM THE WISDOM OF WOLF-THOUGHT! HA HA HA! I DON'T CARE IF THEY HEAR ME! HA HA HA HA!

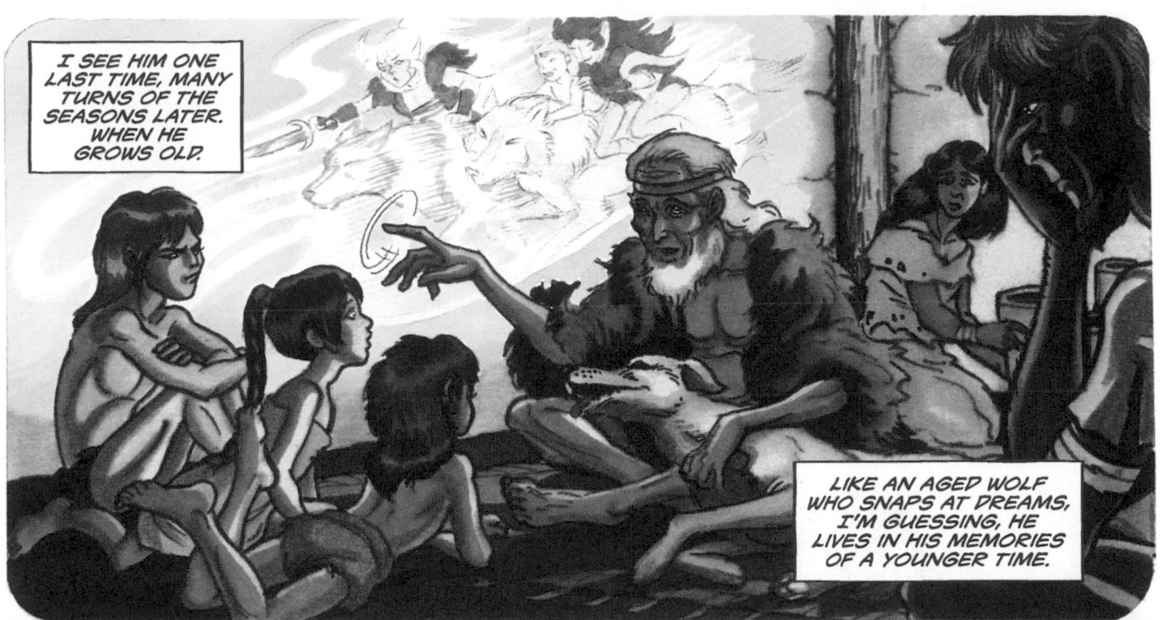
I SEE HIM ONE LAST TIME, MANY TURNS OF THE SEASONS LATER. WHEN HE GROWS OLD.
LIKE AN AGED WOLF WHO SNAPS AT DREAMS, I'M GUESSING, HE LIVES IN HIS MEMORIES OF A YOUNGER TIME.

LUCKY FOR US, THOSE WHO AWAIT HIS DEATH DON'T BELIEVE THEIR FORMER CHIEF'S RAVINGS. HE'S JUST A NUISANCE TO THEM NOW.
PERHAPS, ONE NIGHT, THEY FAIL TO WATCH HIM AS CLOSELY AS THEY SHOULD.

SUDDEN STRENGTH OFTEN COMES TO DYING BEASTS.
IT MUST BE SO FOR SOME HUMANS TOO...

...ELSE HOW COULD **PATCH** GET AS FAR AS THE THORN WALL, AVOIDING CAPTURE?

HE PLUNGES RIGHT THROUGH THE BRIARS, NOT FEELING THEM, CALLING OUT TO US IN OUR TONGUE...
MOTHER!
...CALLING FOR ME!

WHAT ARE WE TO DO?
HE'S GETTING TOO CLOSE!

MOOOOTHER!

HE'S ABOUT TO SHOW HIS PURSUERS THE HOLT, US, EVERY-THING!

FWEEEEET!

"STOP! DANGER!" OH, MY GOOD CUB! HE FREEZES AND FALLS SILENT AS DEATH.

HE'LL NEITHER MOVE NOR SPEAK 'TIL MOTHER SAYS ALL IS SAFE.

THEY MIGHT BE HIS OWN CUBS, THOSE WHO BIND HIM, BLESS HIM, AND LEAVE HIM THERE FOR THE WOLVES.

I CAN'T BLAME THEM.

♫ AYOOOH! AYOOOH! THE PACK HAS FEASTED WELL...LITTLE CUBLINGS SNUGGLE DOWN TO HEAR THE TALES WE TELL... ♪

ONE BRAVE AND HELPFUL LIFE...TWO WORLDS THE BETTER FOR IT. HE DID WELL, MY CUB. HE DID VERY WELL."
STORY BY WENDY AND RICHARD PINI ART BY WENDY PINI

Right of Passage
PANT PANT PANT
SNORT! SNORT! HUFF! SNORT!
STORY BY WENDY AND RICHARD PINI ART BY WENDY PINI

NO YOU DON'T!

YOW! CHOPLICKER...!

EEEEK!

HUH?!
RRRF?!

PUCKERNUTS!

UH-OH!

DIDN'T NOTICE WE WERE WAY OUT HERE IN PLAIN SIGHT! BETTER TAIL IT BACK TO THE WOODS OR FATHER'LL SKIN US SURE!

GASP THE WATER...!

HIGH ONES! IT'S BEEN SIX TURNS OF THE SEASONS...!

?!

"MOTHER... SUNTOP... VENKA...!"
EMBER! HOW DID YOU KNOW TO GREET US HERE?! WE DID NOT SEND!

RAYEK SENSED THERE WERE NO HUMANS ABOUT. IT IS SAFE, FOR NOW.
BUT WHAT ARE YOU DOING HERE, KITLING?
OH...JUST HUNTING!

NEVER MIND THAT! HOW COME THE PALACE IS FLYING AGAIN? DID RAYEK'S MAGIC COME BACK?
IT SEEMS SO.

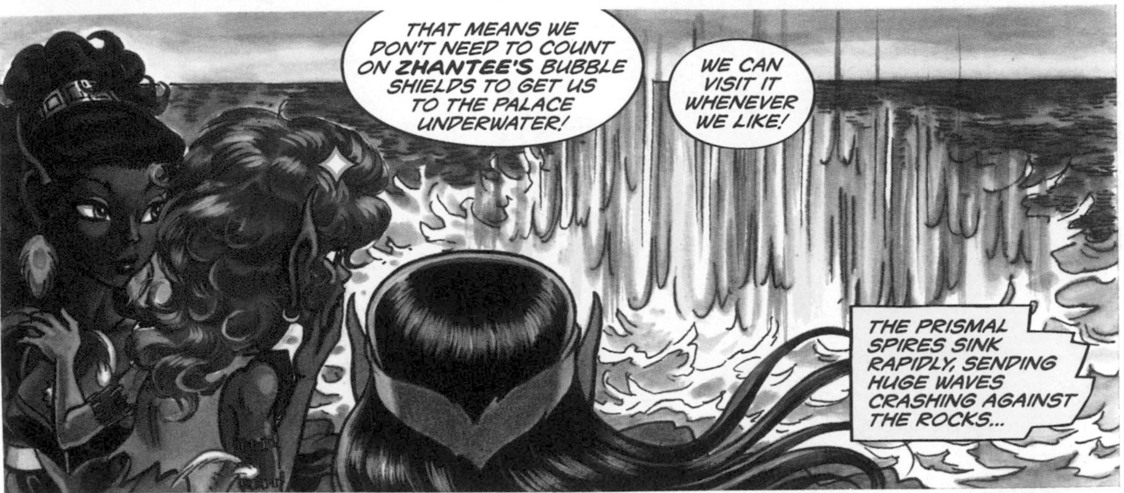
THAT MEANS WE DON'T NEED TO COUNT ON ZHANTEE'S BUBBLE SHIELDS TO GET US TO THE PALACE UNDERWATER!
WE CAN VISIT IT WHENEVER WE LIKE!
THE PRISMAL SPIRES SINK RAPIDLY, SENDING HUGE WAVES CRASHING AGAINST THE ROCKS...

AND WE CAN TRAVEL AGAIN TOO... AS FAST AS SKYFIRE! WE CAN SEE THE WHOLE WORLD!
LET'S JUST SEE ABOUT GETTING BACK TO THE HOLT, ADDLEBIRD!

AH, VENKA! AS MUCH AS I HAVE LOOKED FORWARD TO THIS DAY, I KNOW CUTTER HAS DREADED IT!
YES, THE COMING COUNCIL MAY NOT END HAPPILY.
...OUGHTN'T TO HAVE BEEN ANYWHERE NEAR THE CLIFFS!
OUGHT!
OUGHTN'T!
OUGHT!

SOON, IN THE DEEPMOST PART OF THE FOREST--THE WOLFRIDERS' SECRET HOLT...
NOT ONCE SINCE MY SIRE, RAYEK, LOST HIS DREAM OF SAVING THE HIGH ONES HAS HE ALLOWED HIMSELF REST...OR JOY...OR MERCY.
ON THE DAY HE CHOSE NOT TO MERGE THE PALACE WITH ITS TWIN, HIS POWERS LEFT HIM.
HE'S BEEN BUT A SHADOW OF THE ONE YOU KNEW, HOLDING EKUAR AND ME AT ARM'S LENGTH.
"...LONGING FOR WINNOWILL, WHO LIVES BUT LIVES NOT, MOVES NOT, SENDS NOT...SHE, ALONE, WHO MUST HEAL HERSELF!
"TO THE MARROW OF HIS BONES HE KNOWS... HE KNOWS THE PAIN HE'S CAUSED OTHERS!"
BUT TODAY, WOLFRIDERS, I SAW HIM SMILE!
TODAY THE SCROLL OF COLORS TURNED FOR HIM...
AND THE PALACE ROSE FOR HIM! TODAY HE WANTS TO BEGIN TO MAKE AMENDS.

VENKA'S RIGHT! I WAS THERE!
I'D "GONE OUT" TO TRAIN WITH SAVAH WHEN THE PALACE, WELL, SHIVERED...AND I HAD TO COME BACK IN!
BUT BEFORE I DID, SAVAH CALLED ME!

" 'COME HOME,' SHE SAID, 'WHERE HANDS CAN TOUCH...
" '...AND EYES CAN SEE WITH JOY!

" 'COME HOME TO SORROW'S END!' "

SO YOU MUST!
IT'S LONG...LONG OVERDUE! AND IT'S YOUR RIGHT AS A MAGIC-USER.
OUCH! THAT CAN'T HAVE BEEN EASY!

BE WHAT YOU'RE MEANT TO BE, CUB...
...THOUGH IT'S PAST ME TO GUESS WHAT THAT IS!

WE'VE SPOKEN BEFORE, LIFEMATE. LET WHAT IS SAID NOW SETTLE THE MATTER.
AS SAVAH GUIDES SUNTOP, SO I'VE TRIED TO GUIDE MENDER FROM AFAR.
BUT THE ILLS IN SORROW'S END STILL LIE BEYOND HIS ABILITY TO CURE.
"THE BATTLE TOOK PLACE WELL BEFORE YOUR LONG SLEEP, BELOVED...WHEN YOU HAD NO MEANS TO BRING AID TO THE SUN FOLK...BECAUSE THE GREAT PALACE WAS GONE.
"NOW SOMETHING CAN BE DONE FOR THOSE WOUNDED...BUT NOT READY TO DIE...WHO CHOSE, INSTEAD, TO SLEEP."
I SWEAR I WILL STAY NO LONGER THAN IT TAKES TO HELP MENDER FINISH HIS WORK.
I, TOO, SISTER!
SAY, WHAT'S ALL THIS SQUIRREL CHATTER FOR?! WE'LL ALL GO! I KNOW I'M READY!

THIS *ISN'T* A SWING THROUGH THE BRANCHES OR A LAZY SWIM DOWNSTREAM.

ANY JOURNEY IN THE PALACE IS RISKY! IT'S *RAYEK* WHO MAKES THE CURSED THING FLY AND, SORRY OR NOT, IT'S *RAYEK* WHO TORE US APART ONCE BEFORE!

IF I DIDN'T TRUST *VENKA'S* MAGIC TO KEEP HER SIRE AND THE BLACK SNAKE IN LINE, NO ONE WOULD SET FOOT IN THE PALACE AGAIN!

YOU'RE SAYING... I CAN'T GO...?

I'M SAYING JUST THAT.

WHEW! THIS STORM'S BEEN GATHERING A LONG TIME!

MAYBE I DON'T HAVE THE SAME REASONS...

...BUT I HAVE JUST AS MUCH RIGHT AS SUNTOP TO GO TO SORROW'S END!

THE... COUNCIL...IS... DONE!
NOT 'TIL I'VE HAD MY SAY!

AND YOU'D BETTER HEAR ME OUT OR I'LL...

HEY! HOLD IT!

WHO TAUGHT YOU TO DO THAT, ANYWAY?

YOUR GRANDSIRE... BEARCLAW. WHEN I WAS A CUB I WAS ALMOST AS STUBBORN AS YOU!
WELL, DON'T TRY THAT AGAIN!

A WAYS FROM HERE, BEFORE THE HUMANS DUG IT UNDER, THERE WAS A TREE...
I KNOW...

YOU USED NEW MOON TO MAKE ONE NOTCH FOR EVERY TURN OF THE SEASONS.
LOSING YOU FOR SO LONG...YOU CAN'T KNOW...
SHOW ME! LOCK-SEND AND SHARE WITH ME! PLEASE!

THAT I'LL NEVER DO. NO ELF SHOULD EVER HAVE TO...
LISTEN, EVERY NOTCH IN THAT TREE WAS A DEFIANCE OF THE WAY. WHEN YOU'RE CHIEF, YOU'LL KEEP ONLY TO THE "NOW" OF WOLF-THOUGHT!

FATHER, YOU KNOW BETTER!
EVER SINCE YOU STARTED FINDING NEW ELF TRIBES, THE WAY HAS HAD TO BE STRETCHED AND BENT!
YOU BLAME ME...?

NO! NEVER! BUT DON'T YOU SEE?
BECAUSE OF YOU, THE WAY INCLUDES ALL ELVES AND THE PALACE TOO...AND--AND BEING ABLE TO CHANGE ON THE SPOT!

THEY SAY I HAVE A GIFT FOR THAT. BUT I PAY A PRICE.
LOOKING BEYOND "NOW," SEEING WHAT'S POSSIBLE, MEANS LOOKING BEHIND TOO. IT'S HARD.. VERY HARD...TO FORGET.

QUESTS, WARS, TIME JOURNEYS...
ALL YOU'VE BEEN THROUGH... THAT'S OVER!
IT'S UP TO *YOU* TO PRESERVE THE WAY AS IT WAS...
...BEFORE I MUCKED IT! IT'S UP TO YOU... *HUH?!*
LET ME BREATHE!

LATER...
PART OF IT'S THE LADS, YOU KNOW. SHE'S FULL OF FIERY YOUNG DREAMS.
HMH...! YOU AND AROREE DON'T KEEP JUST TO YOURSELVES. NEXT TO SUNTOP YOU'RE THE YOUNGEST NOW. MAYBE YOU...

...IN A HEARTBEAT, IF EMBER WANTED IT SO!
BUT I'D SAY IT'S NEW FACES SHE CRAVES, MORE THAN YOUTH.
SHE'S NOT GOING TO SORROW'S END.

HEY IN THERE! THIS IS SKYWISE, REMEMBER?!
YOU'LL SIT ON EMBER SO YOU CAN BEAR LEETAH AND SUNTOP'S GOING! BUT YOU CAN GO TOO, ROCK-SKULL! WE'LL GET BY SOMEHOW!

NO.
I DON'T DARE ENTER THE PALACE SO LONG AS RAYEK'S THERE.

THE WOLF IN ME WOULD SEEK HIS THROAT. NOTHING COULD STOP IT.

IT'S NOT FAIR! HOW CAN I KNOW HOW FATHER FEELS WHEN HE WON'T SHARE WITH ME?!
CHOOSE KINDNESS THIS TIME, KITLING. THERE WILL BE OTHER JOURNEYS!

BUT SUNTOP GETS TO GO AWAY NOW! SUNTOP'S BETTER THAN ME BECAUSE HE'S FULL OF MAGIC, RIGHT?!
WELL, GO ON! ALL OF YOU! GO JUMP IN THE SEA, FOR ALL I CARE!

ALL WILL BE DONE IN SUCH HASTE THAT EVEN THE CHANCE HUMAN WITNESS, BLINKING ONCE, COULD NOT SAY JUST WHAT HE SAW.
STARLESS AND MOONLESS, THE LATE NIGHT SKY...RAW AND BITING, THE SALTY BREEZE.

EMBER REFUSES TO ANSWER OUR SENDINGS. WE CANNOT WAIT!

FARE WELL, BELOVED...!
DON'T! PLEASE! JUST GO!

THE MEMORIES RUSH AND OVERLAP LIKE THE ICY BREAKERS BELOW. A SUDDEN, HEART-TEARING FLASH... MIND-SCREAMS OF STOLEN KIN...
I CAN DO THIS... I CAN DO THIS...!

GASP EMBER!
AYOOOOAA-AAAHHHH!

SORRY, EKUAR!
OOOPFF!
UGH!
OUCH!

HEH HEH... HEH HEH HEH
DID YOU SEE THAT?! WHAT A CUB!

HEH HEH HEH
HEE HEE
CHUCKLE
GIGGLE
SNARF

GET YOUR DISRESPECTFUL TAILS BACK TO THE HOLT...!

NOW!

SOON, IN A DARKENED HUT CLAY-ARMORED AGAINST THE BLISTERING DESERT NOON...

IT IS THE GREAT PALACE, **MENDER**...IT UNITES US IN A CIRCLE OF HEALING BEYOND ANYTHING WE COULD ACCOMPLISH SEPARATELY.

WONDERFUL! **OOOOHHH...!**

:SIGH: MOTHER...? H-HOW MANY DAYS...?

NEVER MIND, ***KIMO!*** YOUR FATHER'S SPIRIT *:CHOKE:* REJOICES WITH US!

I SAW THESE WOUNDED WRAPPED BY PRESERVERS AND THOUGHT, "HOW SAD! THEY'LL MISS SO MUCH!" BUT WHEN I HEARD OF CUTTER'S LONG SLEEP, I FELT PULLED TO JOIN HIM AND HIS WOLFRIDERS!
MY DREAMS WERE ONLY OF THIS DAY! BUT THE WAKING TRUTH IS MORE...SO MUCH MORE THAN...
MOTHER'S THE BEST! STILL, SHE'S LUCKY YOU WERE HERE TO HELP HER!
I-I'M GLAD YOU'RE HERE TOO, MENDER! BUT WHY DIDN'T ALL OUR WOLF-KIN SLEEP?

WHY DIDN'T WING AND WOODLOCK AND RAINSONG...?
LIFE WAS FULL FOR MY BROTHER AND PARENTS. THEY WALKED THE PATH TO ITS NATURAL END.

NEWSTAR AND I, YOUR FOREST FOLK...NONE OF US WHO SLEPT COULD GUESS HOW LONG IT WOULD TAKE THE PALACE TO RETURN.
MOTHER AND FATHER DECIDED TO COUNT THE YEARS THIS WAY.

WING TOOK UP WHERE THEY LEFT OFF. BUT BY THEN THE DIFFERENCE IN AGE, HIS FROM THEIRS, MEANT NOTHING. SO...
...SO, AFTER WING, THE SUN FOLK KEPT TRACK OF THE YEARS? THERE'S LOTS MORE PEBBLES IN THEIR JAR THAN IN THE WOLFRIDERS'!

COME! IT'S THE HOW OF LIVING THAT COUNTS, NOT HOW LONG!

YOU'RE DIFFERENT FROM SUNTOP! LEETAH TOLD ME!
YOUR BLOOD'S ALL WOLFRIDER, PURE AND HOT...
SIGH JUST LIKE YOURS!
...JUST LIKE MINE!

WHEN THE GO-BACKS INVADED US TO STEAL THE LITTLE PALACE, I SURPRISED MYSELF! THE WOLF ROSE IN ME AND...
...WELL, MANY OF THE WOUNDS I LATER HEALED, I CAUSED... WITHOUT SHAME! IT WAS GRAND!
THE BALANCE I SEEK WITHIN ME IS POSSIBLE! YOUR MOTHER, THE GREATEST OF HEALERS, AND YOUR FATHER, MIGHTIEST OF WARRIORS, SHINE TOGETHER AS MY GUIDES!
YOU HAVE A FIERCE HALF AND A GENTLE HALF...AND THEY'RE FIGHTING INSIDE YOU! OH, MENDER, I KNOW!
OF COURSE! YOU'RE CUTTER'S CUB...EVERY BIT!
IT'S THE NEXT BEST THING TO MEETING HIM! IF ONLY HE HAD COME TOO!
HUNH! YOU THINK YOUR HEROES ARE PERFECT? WELL, THEY'RE NOT! ESPECIALLY MY FATHER!

EMBER, I-I DIDN'T...
HE'S MEAN! AND UNFAIR! HE FORBADE ME TO COME HERE... FOR NO GOOD REASON!
EMBER, PLEASE...!
I MISSPOKE!
OH, WHAT'S THE USE?!
YOU'RE SO FAR ON HIS SIDE YOU'RE WRAPPED AROUND HIM!
IT IS THE HOTTEST PART OF THE DAY.
EMBER, WAIT!
THE SUN FOLK HAVE REPAIRED TO THEIR UNDERGROUND ROOMS, WHILE CHOPLICKER DOZES IN THE SHADE WITH TOLERANT JACK-WOLVES.

IT'S ALL DIFFERENT! DON'T KNOW MY WAY AROUND!
BUT IT'S SIX TURNS SINCE I WAS HERE! JUST SIX!
MENDER WAS LITTLE... YOUNGER THAN ME!

JARS FULL OF PEBBLES...! NO! IT'S TOO CRAZY!
I KNOW WHERE TO GO!
WAIT!

EMBER!
...BER...
...BER...
...ER...
...ER...
...ER...
EMBER!
...BER...
...BER...

:SOB:
:SOB:
WHAT IS IT? ARE YOU HURT? DON'T MOVE! I'M COMING!
PLEASE SEND! TELL ME WHAT'S WRONG!
BERRR...!

:SOB:
:SOB:
EMBERRR...!
ERR...!
BERRR...!
ERR...!
WHY? :SOB: WHY...?!

AHDRI DIDN'T HAVE TO RESHAPE ALL THE ROCKS AROUND SORROW'S END, DID SHE?!
SHE COULD HAVE LEFT THIS SPOT ALONE! :SNIFF: SHE SHOULD HAVE!
:PANT PANT: THANK THE HIGH ONES YOU'RE ALL RIGHT! BUT WHAT'S...?

RIGHT HERE, THERE WAS A LITTLE TUNNEL. IT LED TO A GLITTER-ROCK FOREST... MY VERY OWN, MY SECRET HOLT...WHEN I USED TO BE A VILLAGER!

SIGH
AHDRI DIDN'T CAUSE THE CAVE-IN THAT CRUSHED YOUR FOREST! TIME DID! IMMENSE TIME!
SOMETHING YOU LOVED... AND EXPECTED TO BE HERE ALWAYS... JUST ISN'T ANYMORE!

THINK HOW MUCH MORE PRECIOUS THAN GLITTER-ROCKS YOU WERE TO CUTTER WHEN...

...WHEN I WAS GONE FOR ONE NIGHT...A NIGHT THAT LASTED AS LONG AS IT TOOK TO FILL THOSE TWO JARS WITH PEBBLES.
POOR FATHER...!

I SAW ONLY MY HEROES IN YOU...NOT YOU AT ALL!
AND YOU... SO BEAUTIFUL...I JUST WANTED TO SHOW YOU OFF TO EVERYONE!

ISN'T THERE SOMETHING... JUST FOR US...?
...A SECRET WE CAN SHARE...?

AH! I SEE IT...! YOUR GLITTERING FOREST!
IT'S OURS! GASP OURS!

LATER, IN SAVAH'S AUDIENCE CHAMBER...
...THE WORTH OF SUCH A SEARCH IS UP TO YOU, VENKA. EVEN BEFORE YOU SLEPT YOU KNEW YOUR MOTHER KAHVI AND TYLDAK WERE MISSING. ALL WE KNOW IS THAT THEY LEFT THE LITTLE PALACE HERE WITH US.
DEAR AHDRI'S ROCK-SHAPING, MEANT OVER THE YEARS TO FORTIFY AND EVEN DISGUISE THE VILLAGE FROM GO-BACKS, HAS PROVED A DETERRENT, RATHER, TO HUMAN INTRUDERS.
THEY ARE SUCH ABLE EXPLORERS, NOW, THAT WINDKIN MUST KEEP CONSTANT VIGIL. SOMEDAY THEY WILL KNOW WE ARE HERE.
WHAT THEN?
THEN, WE GO DEEPER INTO HIDING... OR...BECOME, AT LAST, A TRUE PEOPLE OF THIS WORLD!
THOUGH IT HAPPENED HERE IN THE DISTANT PAST, OUR KIND DID SHED BLOOD OF ITS OWN. WE ARE NOT ABOVE HUMANS.
IS IT TOO MUCH TO HOPE THAT THEY HAVE GROWN ABLE TO MEET US AS FRIENDS?
WELL, IF THEY HAVEN'T, WE HAVE THE GREAT PALACE BACK AND...
...AND WE'RE GOING TO BE VERY SMART ABOUT HOW WE USE IT!

LOOK AT IT!
IT CAN TAKE US ANYWHERE, TO ANY TIME...EVEN TO THE STARS! SOMEDAY WE'LL ALL BE ITS MASTERS!

BUT FOR NOW, ONLY RAYEK CAN MAKE IT FLY. AND EVEN HE ALLOWS HE'S GOT LIMITS!
WE HAVE TO KEEP THINGS SIMPLE! WE HAVE TO GO RIGHT BACK TO THE HOLT!

AND MENDER'S COMING WITH US TO LEARN HOW REAL WOLFRIDERS LIVE!
"REAL," IS IT?

THE WORLD HAS BEEN WITHOUT US WOLFRIDERS FOR TWO FULL JARS' WORTH OF TIME!
THE TREES, THE WATERS, THE MOUNTAINS...EVEN THE HUMANS MISSED US! YOU SHOULD SEE THEIR SYMBOLS!

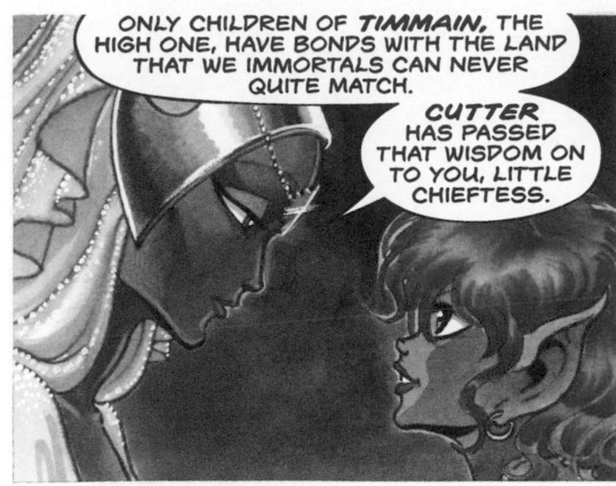
ONLY CHILDREN OF TIMMAIN, THE HIGH ONE, HAVE BONDS WITH THE LAND THAT WE IMMORTALS CAN NEVER QUITE MATCH.
CUTTER HAS PASSED THAT WISDOM ON TO YOU, LITTLE CHIEFTESS.

AND WHENEVER HE PASSES NEW MOON TO ME, I'LL WIELD IT TO HIS HONOR.
WITH ALL MY HEART!

THAT EVENING...
DEWSHINE... SCOUTER...YOU NEVER MEANT TO LIVE HERE SO LONG...
...BUT NOW WE'RE GOING BACK TO THE WOODS! WINDKIN NEARLY FORGOT US WHILE WE SLEPT. SEE THAT HE REMEMBERS US, DART!
SHENSHEN... HAS DECIDED TO STAY!
HOW STRANGE AND WONDERFUL TO KNOW WE HAVE DAUGHTERS AGAIN, BELOVED!

BE HAPPY, CLOUD-HEAD!
BE GOOD, PEST!

GUESS WHAT! I HAVE MAGIC TOO...ALL MY OWN!

"STRANGE AND WONDERFUL..."

...A SEA-SPANNING JOURNEY SO SWIFT THAT **MENDER** HAS BUT MOMENTS TO ANTICIPATE HIS FIRST SCENT OF THE GREEN-GROWING PLACE.

AND...
SEE...? YOU DIDN'T JUST GET MOTHER, SCOUTER, DEWSHINE, AND ME BACK--YOU GOT AN EXTRA! AT LEAST 'TIL HE'S LEARNED ALL HE CAN FROM US!
SOMETIMES WE TEACH, SOMETIMES WE GET TAUGHT... LIKE YOU'VE TAUGHT ME, CUB!

AND NOW THAT I KNOW MENDER, I REALLY UNDERSTAND...I MEAN... ABOUT YOU AND MOTHER.
YOU AND I AREN'T ALIKE AT ALL, ARE WE?
:GIGGLE: NOPE! NOT A BIT!

IN THE WOODS SURROUNDING THE HOLT RULED BY BEARCLAW...
<HEH HEH...OUR WEARY SNAKE-TAIL THOUGHT HE WOULD BE SAFE UP THERE! HE DID NOT KNOW WE COULD CLIMB AS FAST AS HE!>
<SHHH! THE LEAVES ARE THIN! THE THROWING SPACE IS CLEAR! THINK ONLY OF THAT!>
Starfall, Starrise
STORY BY WENDY AND RICHARD PINI
ART BY WENDY PINI
THE SEASONS WILL TURN EIGHT FULL TIMES BEFORE CUTTER, BLOOD OF TEN CHIEFS, IS BORN...

<WHY SO GRIM WITH A TARGET SO EASY?!>
<MY FIRST BLACKSTONE KNIFE SAYS I FELL HIM IN ONE TOSS!>

"<GOTARA BURN IT! MISSED!>"

<...BUT THIS NEXT ONE...>

"<AH!>"

<AFTER SUCH A FALL... HE WALKS AWAY!>
<A DEMON! IT MUST BE!>
"<DEMONS CAN CHANGE SHAPE!>
"<THEY CAN TAKE GREAT PUNISHMENT AND LIVE TO PLAY THEIR TRICKS ANOTHER DAY!>"
ACK! STUFFED DOWN ITS NECK...A WHITE STRIPE'S STINKBAG!
"<BUT WE ARE LIKE THE BEFORE-TIME WARRIOR OUR ELDERS SING OF! WE ARE LIKE DEMONTRICKER! WE WILL COUNT COUP ON THE POINT-EARS!>"

<HEH HEH...YES, TAF! TONIGHT THEY WILL SING OF US AROUND THE FIRE. STONES ARE AS TRUE AS ARROWS IN OUR HANDS!>
<WE ARE THE BEST! WE DISGUISE OUR BODY SMELLS AFTER DEMON-TRICKER'S WAYS...>
<...AND WE DO NOT KILL!>
<WE TAKE TOKENS TO SHAME THE POINT-EARS!>
<BUT... SHOULD WE DO THIS ALONE?>
<ONLY YOU AND I KNOW WHERE A DEMON'S NEST LIES! WE FOUND IT! IT IS OURS BY RIGHT!>
<STILL, WE HAVE SHIRKED FATHER'S HUT TASKS...>
<HAH! HE WILL FORGIVE US!>
<THE WHOLE TRIBE WILL FORGIVE WHEN THEY SEE THAT DEMONTRICKER LIVES AGAIN... IN US!>

AS THE WARM FLUSH OF EVENING REDDENS THE WOODLAND, THE WOLFRIDERS STIR FROM THEIR PEACEFUL DAYSLEEP.

SOFT ELFIN CHATTER, INDISTINCT FROM THE SINGING OF THE NEARBY STREAM, IS SUDDENLY OVERPOWERED BY CHIEF **BEARCLAW'S** HEARTY LAUGHTER.

MORE FOOD FOR YOUR LIFEMATE, **SHALE?! EYES HIGH** IS SO HEAVY WITH CUB NOW...

...SHE'LL EAT AND FALL RIGHT THROUGH THE BOTTOM OF HER NEST!

WELL...AT LEAST THE WIND'S NOT LIKELY TO BLOW HER AWAY!

SHE'S DAYS OVERDUE. CAN'T YOU PERSUADE HER TO RETURN TO THE HOLT, SHALE?
HEH HEH... JOYLEAF THINKS YOU HAVE SOME SAY IN THE MATTER, LAD!
:SIGH:

YOU KNOW HOW IT IS. EYES HIGH IS EYES HIGH.

HAW HAWW!
AND RECOGNITION ISN'T AS COZY AS YOU THOUGHT, EH?

AS IF YOU COULD REMEMBER, OLD BADGER!
WHEN IT HAPPENS TO YOU AND ME, IT'LL BE YOUR LAST TIME! BE SURE OF THAT!

SOON... SOON...WHEN I'M DONE WITH ALL OF YOU, WE'LL BE HIP DEEP IN CUBS!
NOT THAT YOUR RECOGNITION NEEDED PROMPTING, SHALE!
CAREFUL, SIRE RAIN!
I WAS YOUR FIRST TRY, AND LOOK WHAT YOU GOT!

OH, I TRUST I'VE IMPROVED MY HEALER'S SKILLS SINCE THEN, PIKE!
WELL, I'D BEST HURRY!
CHUCKLE

RAIN'S SMILE FADES. HE CANNOT TRULY FORCE RECOGNITION.
BUT THE WOLFRIDERS NEED CUBS. THERE HAVE BEEN CAPTURES AND KILLINGS OF LATE...

...AS EACH DAY THE HUMANS GROW MORE FANATICAL IN THEIR HATRED..
...AND MORE CUNNING IN THE HUNT.
<THERE! IT'S STILL THERE...!>

"<...ATOP THE TALLEST TREE!>"

<MORE MUSK, TAF!>

"<THAT WOLF GUARD WILL NOT ATTACK A THORNY HUMPED MUD PIG!>
"<AND THAT IS JUST WHAT HE WILL SMELL!>

"<NOTHING WILL KEEP US FROM THAT NEST!>"
THE WIND IS UP, LITTLE SKYWISE. SEE? THE CLOUDS RACE PAST THE SUN.
THE SKY WILL SEEM A BOTTOMLES POOL TONIGHT.
YOU'LL BE BORN AS CLOSE TO THE STARS AS YOU CAN BE... JUST AS I PROMISED!

!

BELOVED!

<TWO!>
<TWO FOR COUNTING COUP!>

GOOD! WE'RE STARVING!
IF I CAN'T KEEP BOTH OF YOU FED NOW...
...HOW MUCH WORSE WILL IT BE WHEN **SKYWISE** IS OUT HERE?!

WE'LL KNOW BEFORE DAWN, SHALE.

I'VE DECIDED YOU MAY STAY, IF YOU WISH.
IF I WISH?! YOU KNOW IT'S WHAT I WANT, MORE THAN ANYTHING!

I'VE ALWAYS LIKED BEING ALONE...BUT NOT NOW.
THANK YOU...

GASP

<KNOCK THEM DOWN, BROTHER!>
<WE'LL TAKE THEIR EARS AND SEND THEM RUNNING, NAKED, TO THEIR DEMON PACK!>

WHA...
AAIIIEEE!
GET DOWN!

<HA HAH! THE WIND IS WITH US!>

HURRY! CLIMB DOWN WHERE THE BRANCHES CAN SHIELD Y--UNH!

<THIS IS THE ONE!>
ANH!
SHAAAALE!

SHE DID NOT KNOW SHE WOULD FEEL HIM STRIKE THE GROUND!

ONLY NOW DOES SHE REALIZE THE DEPTH OF THE BOND THAT IS RECOGNITION!

NO, LITTLE SKYWISE... WAIT!

<WHY DOESN'T THE DEMON GET UP?>
<I CARE NOT!>
<HOW DO WE CLAIM OUR TROPHIES WITH THE WOLVES STANDING THERE?>

GASP
KOEI...!

HER SOUL NAME, CALLED, PIERCES HER HEART. SHE RETURNS HIS...
ZASH...? ZASH!
...MY BACK...! DON'T MOVE ME...!

IN TWO KINDS OF AGONY, EYES HIGH SENDS FOR THE WOLFRIDERS...
RUN, BELOVED...!
DON'T STAY...DON'T HOLD THE CUB BACK...

HUMAN HUNTERS, SEEKING TWO ERRANT YOUNG TRIBESMEN...
...HAVE COME UPON A FEAST FOR THEIR GREAT SPIRIT **GOTARA!**

RRAAARRR!
GRRRRR!
EYE... EYES HIGH...! NO!

UNCANNY! UNNATURAL! THESE WERE ONCE **GOTARA'S** BEASTS BEFORE THE POINT-EARED DEMONS CORRUPTED THEM!

EACH VALIANT SPEAR THRUST, EVERY DROP OF BLOOD SPRAYED IS **PLEASING** TO THE MUCH-OFFENDED GREAT SPIRIT.

<THE FANGED ONES ARE SLAIN. NOW, DEMONS...!>
<WAIT!>

<THIS ONE IS OURS!>
OOUUUHHH...!

<LOOK! SHE'S WITH YOUNG!>
<A DOUBLE PRIZE!>

BELOVED...!

<SO, EHOK... TAF...YOU WENT OFF ON YOUR OWN!>

KOEI...!

<BUT IT SEEMS YOU HAD GOOD CAUSE!>

<NEVER HAVE WE OFFERED SUCH A SACRIFICE!>
<THE UNBORN'S SPIRIT WILL TASTE VERY SWEET TO GOTARA!>

<BECAUSE THE CATCH IS YOURS...>

<...YOU TWO SHALL BE HONORED ABOVE ALL OTHER YOUTHS!>

<YOU WERE RIGHT, OLDER BROTHER!>
<THEY FORGAVE US!>

<EHOK...?>

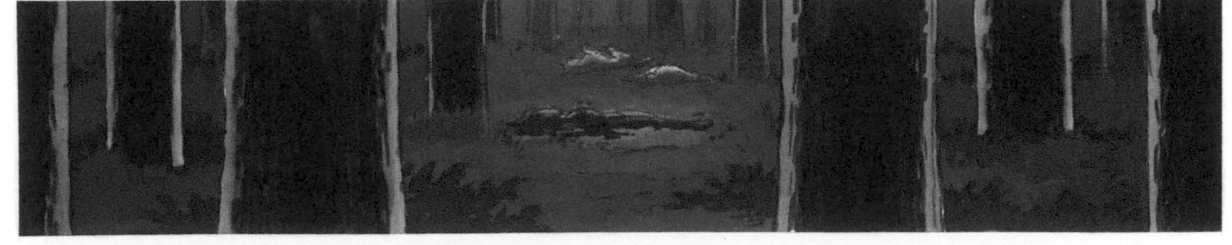

SOON...YET TOO LATE... SCENTS AND TRACKS TELL THE PAINFUL STORY...

LET SHALE LIE IN EYES HIGH'S NEST.
IF SHE STILL LIVES, WE MUST SAVE HER!

BROWNBERRY, FOXFUR, BACK TO THE FATHER TREE!
BUT...
THIS IS MY FAULT! FROM NOW ON NO ONE GOES OFF ALONE!

"AND NEVER AGAIN WILL I RISK MY LIFE-BEARERS IN BATTLE WITH HUMANS!"
<HEEE YAHH!>
<GOTARA!>
<GOTARA!>
NO ANSWER FROM EYES HIGH!
AYE, REDMARK. BUT WHY THE PREPARATIONS? WHY THE DRUMS AND DANCING IF SHE'S ALREADY DEAD?

IN A CEREMONIAL HUT RAISED ONLY FOR THE NIGHT'S RITUAL, EYES HIGH SHUTS HER MIND TO HER TRIBEMATES' SENDINGS.
SHE MUST PROTECT THEM! BEFORE THEY SEE...AND FOOLISHLY TRY TO SAVE HER...SHE MUST DIE!

<HER YOUNG LEAPS INSIDE HER! YET SHE HOLDS BACK! IT IS KILLING HER! HOW CAN SHE...?>
<SHE IS A DEMON!>

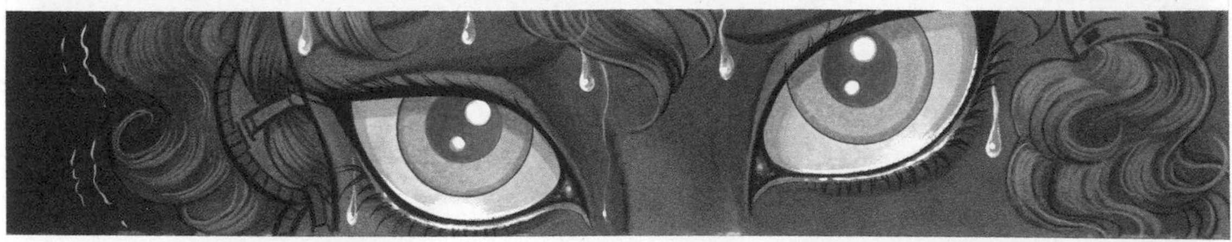

<NO! WHERE IS THE HONOR IN THIS?!>
<WHERE IS THE SPORT? THIS IS NOT DEMONTRICKER'S WAY!>
CALMLY, BROTHER! GOTARA HAS SMILED ON US! DO NOT...>

EHOK!
<OH, NO...! NO!>

TREMBLING WITH TERROR, TAF FOLLOWS HIS BROTHER DOWN TO THE RIVERBANK...
<POOR FOOL, I! SENT TO GUARD THE RAFTS WHILE THE OTHERS SWILL DEMON BLOOD AND SHAKE THEIR SPEARS AT THE MAIDENS!>
<STUPID TASK! WHO WOULD STEAL A FEW STICKS OF WOOD...>
<...STUCK TOGETHER WITH PITCH...? UNGH!>
<GOOD THROW, TAF!>
<FOR THIS THEY WILL BEAT US...OR WORSE!>
<DO NOT FEAR! THE ELDERS SING SONGS OF DEMONTRICKER BECAUSE THEY RESPECT THE RULES OF HIS GAME.>
<WE DO WHAT WE DO IN HIS NAME! THEY WILL UNDERSTAND...AND FORGIVE!>

WAAA... AA-AAAAAH... WAAAHH...!

WAAA... AAAHUH...AAA AAAAHHH...!

YES... **HOWL,** MY WOLFLING! THIS ISN'T AT ALL WHAT I PROMISED YOU!

<LISTEN! THE DRUMS HAVE STOPPED! THE SHOUTS HAVE TURNED ANGRY!>
<THEY KNOW! THEY WILL COME AFTER US!>

AND...
SOMETHING'S MADE THEM FURIOUS!
FOLLOW THEM! IT HAS TO DO WITH EYES HIGH!

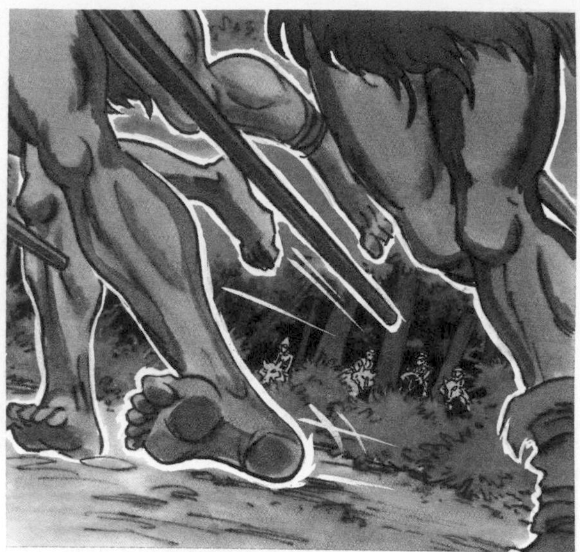

THE RIVER FORKS AND THE BROTHERS CAREFULLY POLE TO THE LEFT.
THE WAY IS WILDER, NARROWER, ROCKIER THAN BEFORE...AN UPSTREAM STRUGGLE.
BUT IT WILL TAKE THEM INTO THE FORBIDDEN TERRITORY OF THE WOLFRIDERS, WHERE THEY CAN LEAVE THE MOTHER AND HER NEWBORN IN PEACE.

EYES HIGH KNOWS THIS PLACE...KNOWS THE YOUTHS SEEK TO AID HER...KNOWS PURSUERS COME...
HER STRENGTH EBBING, SHE BUNDLES SKYWISE IN HER OILED LEATHER CLOAK...

...AND CALLS ONE LAST TIME!
BEARCLAW! COME ALONE... AHEAD OF THE HUMANS! WATCH THE WATER! HURRY!

KAFF KAFF
WHIMPER

FARE WELL, MY CUB! LIVE...! LIVE...!

THE STARS ARE OUT. CAN YOU SEE THEM...?

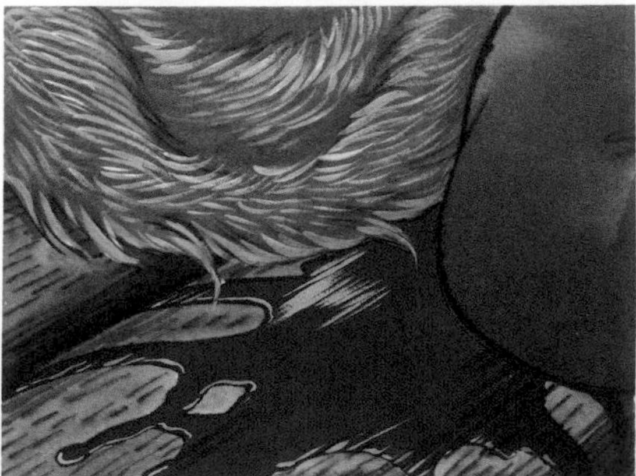

LOOK UP!

DO YOU SEE, SKYWISE...?

...SKYWISE...

SKYWISE!
HEY! DID YOU FORGET ME?
HEH HEH... UH...NO, CUTTER! HOW COULD I FORGET MY OWN SHADOW?!
PUCKERNUTS!

BUT FOXFUR AND I HAVE A LONG WAY TO GO...
...AND STARJUMPER'S RUMP IS SORE. HE CAN'T TAKE EXTRA RIDERS.

NOW, DON'T TELL ANYONE...ESPECIALLY BEARCLAW! THIS IS A SECRET HUNT!
I'M AFTER THE MOST DELICIOUS PREY THERE IS!

DON'T WORRY, SKYWISE! I WON'T TELL! YOU'LL SEE!

"DELICIOUS PREY"...?
WAIT 'TIL YOU SEE MY LURE!

GASP
A FIELD OF DREAM-BERRIES!
FARTHER FROM THE HOLT THAN WE'VE EVER GONE, BUT WORTH THE RISK, EH?
MMMM... OH...OH, LOVEMATE...!
?!?

SKYWISE! THERE'S A HUMAN!
WE'D BETTER RUN!

WAIT! LET'S TAKE A CLOSER LOOK!

BEARCLAW WON'T LIKE THIS!
BEARCLAW THINKS WE'RE FISHING IN GOODTREE'S GLEN!

WHAT'S HE UP TO?

SKYWISE...! AROUND HIS NECK...

...THE ORNAMENT EYES HIGH ONCE WORE IN HER HAIR!

KILLER!

<DIRTY, DOUBLE-CURSED HUMAN!>

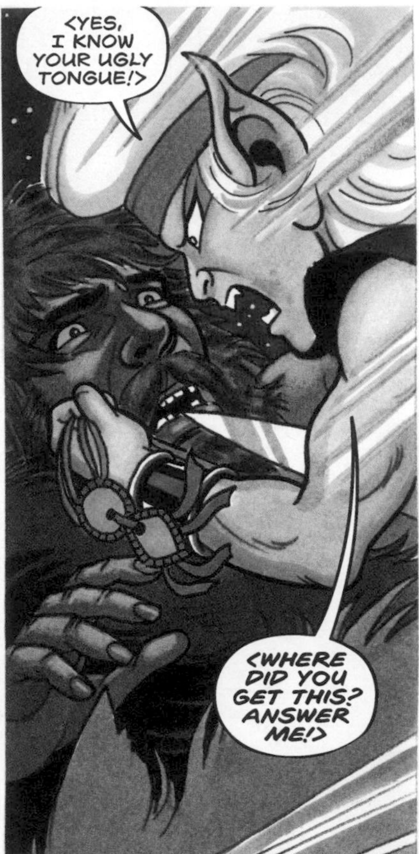
<YES, I KNOW YOUR UGLY TONGUE!>
<WHERE DID YOU GET THIS? ANSWER ME!>

<I...UH...>

<SPEAK, FILTH! IT WAS MY MOTHER'S!>

<YOU...! I--I KNOW YOU!>

<THERE WAS MUCH BIRTH BLOOD. WE COULD NOT KEEP HER ALIVE...>
<...THOUGH WE TRIED!>

<TRIED... TO HELP A "DEMON"?>
<WHAT TROLL DUNG ARE YOU HANDING ME?>

<BELIEVE MY WORDS! THE TRUTH IS TOO TERRIBLE TO FORGET!>

"<WE WERE CAUGHT TRYING TO HIDE HER BODY, MY BROTHER AND I.>"
<THE CEREMONY OF SACRIFICE HAS BEEN MOCKED! DEFILED!>
<WE SHALL ALL KNOW GOTARA'S WRATH!>

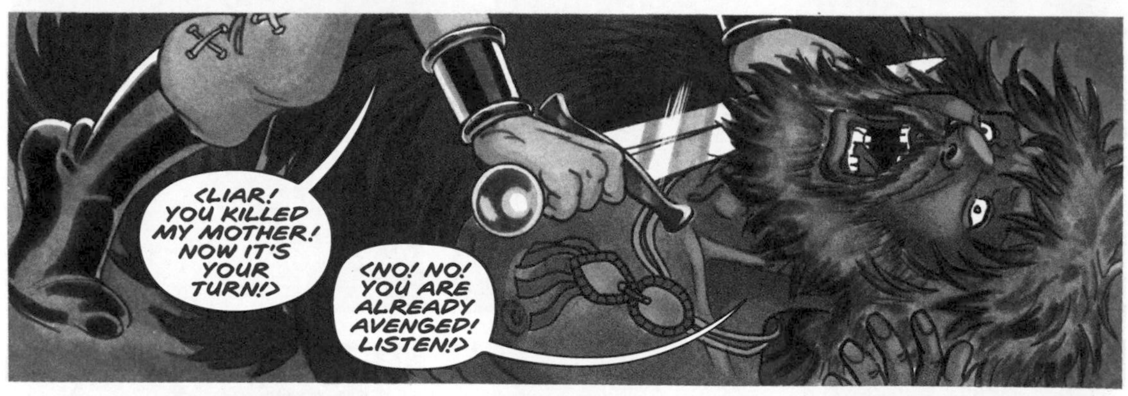
<LIAR! YOU KILLED MY MOTHER! NOW IT'S YOUR TURN!>
<NO! NO! YOU ARE ALREADY AVENGED! LISTEN!>

"<WE WERE MADE TO DRAW LOTS!>
"<MY BROTHER LOST!>"

<TAF!>
<BUT... YOU SAID... THEY WOULD FORGIVE!>

"<I WAS FORCED TO WATCH...AS TAF TOOK YOUR MOTHER'S PLACE ON THE PILLAR OF SACRIFICE!>"

<THIS RING OF STONES...IS HIS LOWLY GRAVE. THE GROUND IS NOT SACRED TO **GOTARA.**>
<**TAF'S** SPIRIT IS FOREVER LOST IN THE DARK!>
<THIS IS NO TROPHY... BUT A SYMBOL OF MY GRIEF AND SHAME!>

GASP

LOVEMATE...?

Daughter's Day

RAYEK...
HAS FAILED...

...FAILED TO PREVENT THE HIGH ONES' ACCIDENT...

...FAILED TO PREEMPT ALL THOSE VOICES... THOSE HE FIRST HEARD SCREAMING PAINFULLY THROUGH **SUNTOP'S** MIND... CALLING THROUGH TIME...
...FAILED TO INSPIRE HIS PEOPLE TO SEEK A HIGHER AND BETTER WAY OF LIFE.

AND NOW HE CAN NO LONGER INSPIRE EVEN THEIR TRUST.

SARAH BYAM - WORDS
PAUL ABRAMS - PENCILS
CHARLES BARNETT - INKS
PATY - COLORS
WENDY PINI - EDITOR

PERHAPS HE HAS SIMPLY LOST FAITH IN HIMSELF...
HE FEELS TRAPPED IN HIS CRUDE, HEAVY BODY... DRY AS A SQUEEZED, BITTER FRUIT...
...WITHOUT MAGIC!
HE CANNOT LIFT THE PALACE OF THE HIGH ONES...
HE CANNOT TURN THE SCROLL OF COLORS...
HE CANNOT EVEN FLOAT HIMSELF A FINGER'S LENGTH ABOVE THE FLOOR.

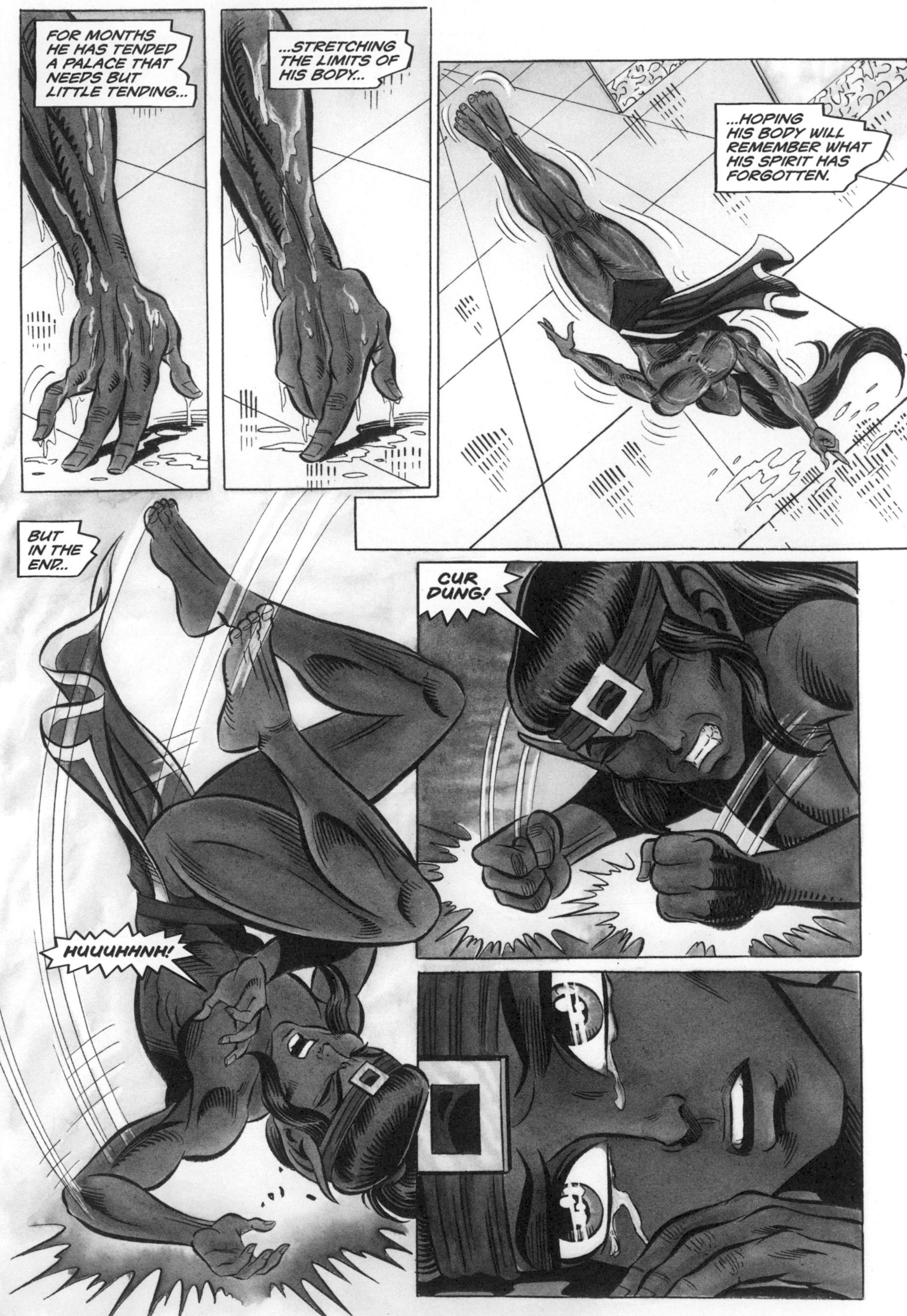
FOR MONTHS HE HAS TENDED A PALACE THAT NEEDS BUT LITTLE TENDING...
...STRETCHING THE LIMITS OF HIS BODY...
...HOPING HIS BODY WILL REMEMBER WHAT HIS SPIRIT HAS FORGOTTEN.
BUT IN THE END...
CUR DUNG!
HUUUHHNH!

I LOVE YOU.

I UNDERSTAND YOU.

AND I AM AS HELPLESS AS YOU ARE.

A WALL OF SEAWATER, HELD FIRMLY BACK BY THE PALACE'S AURA, IS YET PENETRABLE...
SO MUCH TO MEND...SO MUCH TO PUT RIGHT.
DO YOU FEEL SO UNWELCOME THAT YOU MUST ERASE THE LEAST TRACE OF YOURSELF, BROWNSKIN?
IF THE GREATER HARM I HAVE DONE CANNOT BE CLEANED UP--
--AT LEAST I CAN TEND TO THIS.
I HAVE TO DO SOMETHING, EKUAR!
SIGH
WHY NOT DO SOMETHING CONSTRUCTIVE, THEN?
VENKA! ZHANTEE!

COME UP INTO THE SUNSHINE, FATHER!
THE NEW-GREEN HAS SPRUNG--
--AND IT WAS WHITE-COLD THE LAST TIME YOU VENTURED OUT!
AYE! AND SOME OF THE WOLFRIDERS PELTED ME WITH SNOW STONES!
CAN YOU BLAME THEM?
NO...
...BUT, ALL THE SAME, I THINK I SHALL REMAIN DOWN HERE.
WHAT IF WE TOLD YOU THE OTHERS WERE AWAY, TRACKING A NEW HERD?
OH?
MOST OF THEM. A FEW STAYED BEHIND.
LEETAH STAYED BEHIND!

HOW... IS SHE?
PRETTY AS A BLOSSOM AND TWICE AS FRAGRANT!
BUT YOU WON'T EVEN GET A WHIFF OF HER SWEETNESS IF YOU STAY DOWN HERE MOLDING!

COME JOIN THE LIVING, FATHER! COME HUNT WITH ME!

MY MAGIC IS SPENT, VENKA... I--I CANNOT HUNT!

REDLANCE ASSURES ME THESE WILL PULL FOR THE GREENEST BEGINNER!
SURELY YOU WILL TRY WHAT A WOLFRIDER CUB HAS MASTERED!

WELL... LET NO ONE SAY THERE WAS SOMETHING I WAS AFRAID TO TRY!

THAT'S THE RAYEK I KNOW AND ADMIRE!
ADMIRE...?
YOU THINK I'VE BEEN COMING DOWN HERE BECAUSE I FEEL SORRY FOR YOU?
I THOUGHT YOU MORE CLEVER THAN THAT!
AS THE LITTLE PARTY FLOATS TO THE SURFACE, SHIELDED BY ZHANTEE'S MAGIC BUBBLE, RAYEK TURNS.
THE PALACE FADES, SILENT AND GLIMMERING, INTO THE SUNLESS DEEP.
HOW I LONG TO TAKE YOU WITH ME, WINNOWILL...MY SOUL'S SISTER. IT IS HARD TO ENDURE ZHANTEE'S CHARITY...
...HARDER STILL TO ENDURE PITY, SHOULD IT COME.

YOU SEE? IT IS A BEAUTIFUL DAY!
:GASP:... NEVER THOUGHT I WOULD SHRINK FROM THE SUN!
YOU HAVE BEEN UNDERWATER A LONG TIME, FATHER.
"FATHER"... HOW EASILY YOU SAY THAT!
YOUR MOTHER WOULD NOT HAVE APPROVED!
SHE WAS PROUD... LIKE YOU!
KAHVI WAS NOTHING LIKE ME!
OH? SHE HATED NEEDING OTHERS...
SHE WAS SKILLED AND STRONG...
AND YOU TRACK ALMOST AS WELL AS SHE DID!
VENKA... YOUR MOTHER HAD A RESTLESS BODY. I HAVE A RESTLESS SPIRIT.

AND SOMEHOW--
PRAISE THE HIGH ONES--
WE MADE YOU! BUT I
AM STILL NOT CERTAIN
HOW!
YOU KNOW...
KAHVI COULD ALSO
BE GENTLE NOW
AND THEN...
FORGIVE
ME. I DID
NOT MEAN
TO SNAP.

BUT
I RATHER
EXPECTED
YOU'D RESENT
ME, AS YOUR
MOTHER MUST--
IF SHE STILL
LIVES!
I KNOW MY
OWN NAME. I
NEED RESENT
NO ONE!
WHAT?
HAVE YOU EVER
SEEN A CUB PICK A
FIGHT TO PROVE IT
IS NO LONGER A
CUB?
AYE...
WOLVES
FIGHT.
SO?

THOSE WHO KEEP ON
FIGHTING THROUGH THE
MANY SEASONS ARE
TRYING TO PROVE
THEIR POSITION.
I KNOW
WHO I AM...
THAT IS
ALL.
I SEE.
I AM BEGINNING
TO LIKE WHO
YOU ARE, VENKA!

AND
I...YOU!
EH...?!
UH...

I--I'M ALSO
BEGINNING TO LIKE
TRACKING THIS
BUCK!
THERE!
SEE
HIM?

HE SEEMS TO HAVE WANDERED FROM THE HERD.
GOOD! AN OUTCAST IS FAIR GAME FOR US!
IT IS THE TIME OF JOINING...! HIS BLOOD BOILS! SEE HOW HE SHARPENS HIS HORNS, PREPARING FOR A CHALLENGE!
ARE YOU SURE THAT IS THE ONE YOU WANT, FATHER?
THE SCENT FILLS RAYEK'S NOSTRILS. WITHIN HIM, THE LONG-DOZING HUNTER AWAKENS.
AYE! THE VERY ONE!

THE THIRST FOR WORTHY OPPONENTS...THIS, TOO, YOU SHARE ALIKE WITH KAHVI!
YOUR BARB HITS HOME!

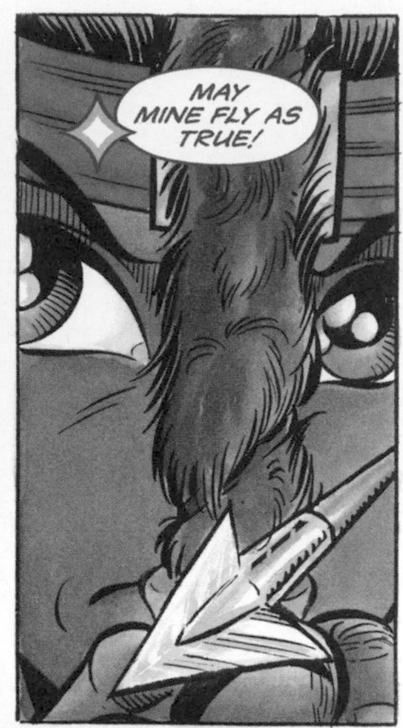
MAY MINE FLY AS TRUE!

THE YOUNG STAG RATTLES HIS ANTLERS, SENSING DANGER.

ZHAANG

ER-O-O-
OU-OU!
HE--HE SCREAMED!
HAAA-AAAH!
UNNH!
SORRY...IT HAS BEEN A WHILE. I AM OUT OF PRAC--
HURRY! HE'LL GET AWAY!
HIS CRY... SO LIKE AN ELF'S! SO HURT!
WHAT DID YOU EXPECT?! COME ON!

THE STAG BLEEDS HEAVILY. THE TRAIL IS EASY.
BUT HE IS STRONG ENOUGH TO OUTPACE THE PARTY BY A GOODLY DISTANCE--AND FOR A GOODLY WHILE.
PUFF PUFF PUFF RIDICULOUS!

A WORTHLESS WILD-ZWOOT CHASE! IT IS TIME WE--
WUU-UP!

DON'T GIVE UP, RAYEK! WE'LL CATCH HIM!
GIVE UP?! WHO SUGGESTED THAT?!
TCH!

HUFF HUFF HUFF SNIFF SNIFF

BNAAAAGHHH

PANT PANT HOOUUUFF?!

SHORTLY...
HE WAS HERE!
PUFF PUFF
WITH CASUAL GRACE, ZHANTEE AND VENKA CLEAR THE STREAM.
HOWEVER...
EEEYUK! SLIMIER THAN A LEATHER-WING'S CAVE! WHAT'S HAPPENED HERE?!
THE HUMANS HAPPENED!
IT IS NO LONGER POSSIBLE TO DRINK DOWNSTREAM FROM THEIR VILLAGE.
THEY MAKE NO USE OF THEIR DROPPINGS TO EXCHANGE TALES AS WOLVES DO.
THE HUMANS EXPECT THE WATER TO CARRY THEIR FILTH AWAY--
--AND YET, SOMEHOW, STAY CLEAN.

RAYEK'S FIRST CRAWL UP THE SLIPPERY BANK IS...
...UNSUCCESSFUL.

HERE! TAKE MY HAND!

THANKS... I NEED NO HELP!

ZHANTEE... I SAID I **DON'T NEED--**
GO ON, FATHER!

AMONG THE WOLFRIDERS, WHAT IS NEEDED IS FREELY GIVEN...
...AND FORGOTTEN.

...M-MUST KEEP UP...!
PANT PANT PANT

...WON'T BE... SHAMED... AGAIN...!

AAA-OW!

IT'S ALL RIGHT, RAYEK! HE'LL SLOW DOWN SOON ENOUGH!
GASP GASP

HE'S BLEEDING TOO MUCH TO RUN ALL DAY!
BUT...HE'S SUFFERING!
THAT'S TRUE.
NOT GOOD ENOUGH!

ALREADY AT THE LIMIT OF HIS ENDURANCE, RAYEK CONTINUES THE CHASE.
...STAG...CRASHED THROUGH THIS STICKER BUSH...
IT IS REDLANCE'S THORN WALL NEAR THE WOLFRIDERS' HOLT. THE LIVING NEEDLES BITE INTO RAYEK'S FLESH, WARNING HIM TO GIVE UP--NOW!
AAAIIEE!
HIS HEART POUNDS, DROWNING OUT ALL OTHER SOUNDS.
HIS LEGS BURN. IT IS A NEW FEELING FOR ONE SO LONG DEPENDENT ON MAGIC.
SUDDENLY...WHEN RAYEK CAN STUMBLE NOT ONE STEP FARTHER...
HUFF HUFF HUFF
PANT WHEEZE HELLO, BROTHER...!

THIS IS NOT TO BE THE NEAT AND PAINLESS KILLING OF EARLIER TIMES--WHEN RAYEK USED THE POWER OF HIS STARE TO LULL THE PREY INTO A MAGICAL HALF SLEEP.
LET HIM GO! ≈PANT PANT≈ I CAN'T--
I-I'D RATHER TEND HIS WOUNDS... THAN FINISH HIM OFF!
TOO LATE FOR THAT, FATHER. HE KNOWS THE GAME... AND REGRET IS NOT PART OF IT.
HE CANNOT RUN--BUT HE CAN FIGHT! CAN'T YOU FEEL THE RAGE IN HIM, VENKA?
HE WANTS TO LIVE! HOW CAN I--?
HOW CAN YOU LEAVE HIM HALFWAY BETWEEN, RAYEK?
HIGH ONES FORGIVE ME...!

RRRAAAUUGH!
YAAAH!
GASP
THE FIGHT LASTS LONGER THAN IT SHOULD. RAYEK'S HEART IS NOT IN IT.
VENKA AND ZHANTEE KNOW HE MIGHT EASILY ASK THEIR AID, BUT...
HE LIVES AS THE WOLFRIDERS LIVE...FIGHTS AS THEY FIGHT!
THE PAIN I DEAL HIM BY HAND...IS NO MORE HONORABLE...THAN THAT I DEALT THEM BY MAGIC.

FATHER, IF YOU LET THE STAG KILL YOU, WE MUST FINISH HIM, ANYWAY!
SHE CALLS HIM FROM THE SHAMEFUL SHADOWS OF A GAME THAT SHOULD NEVER HAVE BEEN PLAYED...
:COUGH COUGH:
...TOWARD THIS GAME'S PROPER END...TOWARD LIFE!
BUT IS HER CALL ENOUGH?
VENKA! WE HEARD THE RUCKUS WAY UP IN THE TREETOPS! WHAT--
SHHH!
AT LAST, ONE SIMPLE THING--
--JUST ONE--
--JARS THE PALACE'S NEARLY BROKEN MASTER FROM ALL OTHER CONCERNS--
--PAIN!
AAAGH!
SNORT SNORT
HUNNNNH!

EQUAL.
ANGRY.
FIERCE.
TWO BEINGS LOCKED IN AN ANCIENT DANCE--
--EACH PROVING HIS WILL TO LIVE AGAINST THE OTHER.
NO PITY.
NO QUARTER.
NO REGRETS!

K-K-HUUUU-UUKK!
MOMENTS LATER, WHEN THE LAST SPASM HAS EBBED..
I...AM... ALIVE!
AYOOOOOAAAAHHHH

AND..
SHOWING OFF AGAIN, OLD FRIEND?
...UUUNNNHH... LEETAH...?! OOW!
BE STILL, WHILE I MEND THIS HOLE IN YOUR THIGH!

DIDN'T THINK YOU HAD IT IN YOU, RAYEK!
NIGHTFALL, WILL--WILL YOU AND THE OTHERS... HONOR THIS STAG--
:AHEM:
--AND SHARE HIS MEAT WITH ME?

I WATCHED CUTTER SUFFER THROUGH WHAT YOU DID TO HIM!
SO YOU'VE TASTED FIRST BLOOD, AND NOW YOU'RE ONE OF US?
NO! I WON'T EAT YOUR KILL!

PLEASE... WAIT!
I ONLY WANTED TO...
...SHARE...!

YOU WON'T WIN THEM OVER ALL AT ONCE, FATHER. BUT I'M PROUD OF YOU.
HNH! NEVER EXPECTED TO HEAR THAT FROM MY OWN CHILD.
THANK YOU...
...DAUGHTER!

The Enemy's Face
"WHEN I WAS BORN, THEY SAY, CHILD MOON STOOD FOR A SHORT TIME BETWEEN THE DAYSTAR AND OUR VILLAGE. THE FLOODS HAD NOT COME IN SEVERAL YEARS...AND THE HEAT HAD BAKED MUCH OF THE LIFE-GIVING SPIRIT FROM THE SOIL.
"CHILD MOON'S SHADOW ACROSS THE DESERT GAVE THE SUN FOLK A MOMENT'S RESPITE...AND HOPE."
HE IS HERE! THE CHILD OF THE ROCKS!
DO LET ME SEE! I HAVE NEVER SEEN A BABY BEF-- GASP
AND YOU, SUN-TOUCHER... YOU TOO SEE... HOW PERFECT HE IS?
MORE THAN THAT, JARRAH...
STORY: SARAH BYAM & WENDY PINI SCRIPT: WENDY PINI ART: PAUL ABRAMS
INKS: CHARLES BARNETT COLORS: PATY LETTERS: NATE PIEKOS

I SEE THAT, LIKE CHILD MOON, **RAYEK** SHALL HAVE REPEATED OCCASIONS TO COME BETWEEN US AND HARM.
HIS IS THE SHADOW PATH.
WHEN THE LIGHT IS TOO STRONG, THE SHADOW INTERVENES AND PROTECTS.
SEEK NOT TO OVERRULE THE LIGHT, YOUNG RAYEK. BE CONTENT TO SHARE THE GLORY AND KEEP THE BALANCE.

"MOST DAYS MY PARENTS TOILED FROM DUSK 'TIL MIDMORN. THEN THEY SLEPT. IT WAS SO FOR ALL THE VILLAGERS."
GREAT SUN, CHILD! GO INSIDE!
WE CANNOT PLAY NOW!

KITLING, TRY TO UNDERSTAND! THE GARDENS MUST COME FIRST!

"I HAD NO GIFT FOR TILLING THE SOIL... AND LITTLE LOVE FOR ITS MEAGER YIELD."
SQUATNEEDLE ROOT IS ALL WE HAVE TO SHARE TONIGHT!
YIICHH!
HEH HEH HEH...WHAT A FACE!

YOU DID NOT HELP US PLANT, MY SON. BE CONTENT WITH WHAT YOU RECEIVE.

"BE CONTENT... **HAH!**

"NEVER DID WORDS FALL ON LESS RECEPTIVE EARS!

"I WAS A NATURAL HUNTER.

"AND EARLY ON I LEARNED BY CHANCE--

"--THAT THE TASTE OF MEAT WAS PLEASING.
"NO ONE TAUGHT ME WHAT WAS NECESSARY.

"I HAD THE WILL... AND THE STOMACH TO LEARN ON MY OWN."

UM...FAIR FIGHT, RIGHT? I WON, SO--
--YOU AND YOUR KIN MUST COME WITH ME!

GASP

"TO MY SURPRISE, MY PARENTS ACCEPTED THE BLOOD GIFT."
YOU KILLED NOT FROM CRUELTY, BUT FROM HUNGER. ANIMALS LIVE THAT WAY. AND IN HARD TIMES, SADLY, SO MUST WE.
BUT WHERE WE HESITATED, YOU CHOSE BRAVELY, RAYEK.

"THEIR PRAISE FELT GOOD. I WISHED TO **GO ON** FEELING GOOD.

"TRUE TO MY NAME, I FELT MORE AT HOME AMONG THE SAND-SMOOTHED LEDGES AND CRAGS THAN IN MY FAMILY HUT.

"AS FOR HUNTING, MY PREY AT FIRST WAS SMALL--THE SMALLER, THE CRAFTIER.

"BUT ONE DAY THE BATTLE OF WITS BECAME--

"--A BATTLE OF NATURAL WEAPONS!"

AAOOOWW!
"TINY TEETH AND CLAWS AGAINST--

"--WHAT?!"

SO MANY!
GASP LOOK!

"SOME STRANGE POWER...THE SORT I HAD ONLY SEEN SAVAH USE...WAS RISING INSIDE ME."
WE ALL GROW STRONG FROM YOUR GIFTS OF DRIED MEAT, CHILD. SO SKILLED, SO YOUNG! HOW?

"I KEPT IT SECRET."
OH, IT--IT IS EASY, MOTHER OF MEMORY! SHARP EYES AND QUICK HANDS ARE ALL I NEED, YOU SEE!

AAH-HMMM...

"BY MY TENTH YEAR, SORROW'S END HAD YET TO SEE ITS FULL MEASURE OF RAIN.
"EVERYONE DEPENDED ON ME.

"ON MY OWN I HAD MASTERED BOTH SPEAR AND KNIFE. AND I WAS EAGER FOR GREATER CHALLENGES IN THE HUNT."
RRREEEE!

"BUT OTHERS WHO DWELT AMONG THE ROCKS HUNGERED TOO."
GRRRRR
GRROOOOWLL
"IT WAS THEY WHO FLUSHED THE BRISTLE BOARS. AND THEY INTENDED TO SHARE...NO MORE THAN I DID."

AWAY, JACKALS! OR I'LL SLASH YOUR UGLY EYES OUT!

"I LEAPT FOR HIGHER GROUND...

"BUT..."
AAAGGHHH!
SNAARLL

NNNH!
WH-I-I-I-NE!

"MY DISABLING STARE STARTLED THEM... STARTLED ME!"
"AS I NEEDED IT, THE POWER CAME TO ME FULL FORCE!
PANT PANT
WHIMPER

"CHANCE CREATED...
"...CHANCE SEIZED!"

NO! FORGET ME, YOU STUPID SACK OF TEETH!
YIIIPE!
GRRR!

"SO I LOST MY SPEAR... AND MY FIRST LARGE KILL...
"...BUT KEPT MY LIFE!"

:PANT PANT:
...UUUNNNHH...
KREE KREE KREE
CHIRRUP CHIRRUP

"AND SOON..."
I WILL FETCH TOORAH!
HURRY! THE WOUNDS ARE DEEP!
:HSSS: I-I AM ALL RIGHT!

"TOORAH WAS GOOD WITH HER SALVES AND GOLDEN NEEDLES.
"I KNEW NOTHING, THEN, OF A HEALER'S ABILITIES BUT HERS--

"--WHICH WERE LIMITED. MY ARM MENDED, BUT HUNG DEAD AT MY SIDE THEREAFTER."
HOOWWOO...HOOOW...WOO...
CURSED, MANGY BEASTS! THE MOUNTAINS ARE MINE!
I WILL RID THEM OF EVERY LAST ONE OF YOU! I SWEAR IT!

"THE BONDS BETWEEN MY PARENTS AND MYSELF GREW WEAKER DAY BY DAY. I NO LONGER NEEDED THEIR CARE. AND OUR INTERESTS WERE AS SHARPLY DIVIDED AS THE SANDS FROM THE SKY."
RISE, SPEAR... RISE INTO MY HAND!
"IN SECRET, I CONTINUED TO EXPERIMENT WITH THE MYSTERIOUS MAGIC AT MY COMMAND."

HAH! YOU GOT MY ARM, JACKALS, BUT I WILL GET YOU!
MY SPEAR WILL FLY FROM ONE THROAT TO THE NEXT--GUIDED BY ME--FROM THE ROCKS HIGH ABOVE YOU!

THE OLD POWERS WELL UP IN ONE OF US SO RARELY, CHILD...
:GASP: SAVAH! YOU...?!
...IT SEEMS A PITY TO WASTE THEM ON ACTS OF VENGEANCE.

COME LEARN FROM ME, RAYEK. YOU NEED NOT STRIVE ALONE TO MASTER YOUR MAGIC.
TOGETHER WE WILL SEEK THE LIMITS OF YOUR ABILITIES--

IF, INDEED, LIMITS THERE BE!
BUT-- BUT THE SUN FOLK...WILL NOT RESPECT ME AS A GREAT HUNTER--

--IF THEY FIND OUT I HAVE USED MAGIC ALL ALONG! THEY WILL THINK I AM STRANGE!
DO YOU THINK ME STRANGE, LITTLE ONE...? DO YOU?
NO!

BUT YOU ARE THE MOTHER OF MEMORY! THAT IS DIFFERENT!
COME...! COME BE MY PUPIL. DO IT FOR YOU...NOT FOR WHAT OTHERS MAY THINK OF YOU!

TOORAH...? WHAT...?

"THERE IS NOTHING SAVAH HAS ASKED OF ME...OR COULD EVER ASK...THAT I COULD EASILY REFUSE."

AH, SUN TOUCHER! WELCOME! THE LAD HAS BEEN FLOATING THREE TOYS IN THE AIR SINCE I ARRIVED! IT IS A WONDROUS SIGHT!

"SHE TOOK ME IN...BECAME MY MOTHER IN A TRUER SENSE THAN SHE WHO BORE ME. FOR ONCE I FELT SUPPORTED BY THOSE WHO COULD BEST UNDERSTAND ME."

MMMMMPH!
CAN'T...DO IT... ANY LONGER! ***UPH!***

SPLENDID! YOUR ENDURANCE GROWS DAILY!
BUT WHAT USE IS JUGGLING DOLLS, SAVAH?
WELL, AT THE VERY LEAST, YOU HAVE THE CHOICE TO GATHER THEM UP WITH ONE HAND...OR NONE!

YOU MEAN LIKE THIS?
:GASP: THE CUP! I SHALL NEVER GET USED TO THINGS FLYING ABOUT THIS WAY!

AND WHAT IS THE DIFFERENCE, DEAR AHDRI, BETWEEN A FLYING CUP AND THE THINGS YOU HAVE SO OFTEN SEEN ME DO?
WHY, NOTHING REALLY, MOTHER OF MEMORY, EXCEPT--

WOOO!
:GIGGLE:

HEH HEH HEH...

POOR RAYEK! HE FANCIES YOUNG AHDRI, BUT I FEAR HE WILL ALWAYS LACK THE CONFIDENCE--
--TO DO MORE THAN TEASE HER! HIS ARM...

ONE'S BODY NEED NOT BE PERFECT FOR ONE TO BE WHOLE.
IF ANYONE CAN TEACH HIM THAT LESSON, IT IS YOU...MY VERY OLD FRIEND!

...VERY OLD...AND BELOVED...FRIEND!
OHHH...! G-GREAT SUN! TOORAH...?!
!?!

ANATIM...!
SO...AFTER SO LONG...IT IS TO BE YOU!
...YOU, TOORAH!
ANATIM!

"WHAT SUDDEN BOLT OF SKYFIRE STRUCK BLIND SUN TOUCHER AND TOORAH, SUCH ANCIENT COMPANIONS, SPARKING THEIR *RECOGNITION?*
"FROM THAT DAY, 'SOUL MEETS SOUL WHEN EYES MEET EYES' TOOK ON A NEW MEANING.
"I WAS FASCINATED. SAVAH EXPLAINED THAT SOMEONE YOUNG--LIKE ME--WAS COMING: A DAUGHTER! BETTER STILL...A TRUE HEALER."
SEE HOW LIGHT IS TOORAH'S STEP! HOW SHE SHINES WITH PERFECT HEALTH!
LITTLE *LEETAH* IS ALREADY AT WORK!
"LEETAH...
"HER NAME SANG IN MY HEART AND HEAD. AFTER A YEAR PASSED--
"SHE AND I MET--
"--FOR THE FIRST TIME.
"AND AFTER A NEARLY ENDLESS WAIT FOR THE PASSAGE OF ANOTHER YEAR...THE HARVEST CAME!
"LEETAH WAS BORN TO THE MUSIC OF A GENTLE THUNDER SHOWER PATTERING ON THE ROOF OF HER FAMILY HUT.
"HER FIRST SOUND MADE, THEY SAY, WAS A GURGLE OF LAUGHTER. MY YEARS, THEN, WERE EIGHT AND FOUR.

"SOON THE FLOODS CAME IN EARNEST. THE DRY TIMES WERE FINALLY GONE.
"I SAW MY FIRST FULL-OUT FESTIVAL OF FLOOD AND FLOWER. THE UNFAMILIAR COLORS OF THE WILD DESERT BLOOMS DAZZLED ME BLIND!
"AS FOR LEETAH, THE SUN FOLK MADE SUCH A TO-DO OVER THE GOOD FORTUNE BROUGHT WITH HER BIRTH, I COULD BARELY GET NEAR HER.
"BEING TOTALLY IGNORED WAS ALSO A NEW EXPERIENCE.
"LIKE IT OR NOT, MY PLACE AT THE CENTER OF ATTENTION HAD BEEN USURPED..THOROUGHLY!"
HOO-OO! HOO! HOO!
BE PATIENT! YOU WILL GET YOUR ZWOOT WHEN I AM READY!
"SOMEHOW-- AND JUST HOW, BELIEVE ME, I KNOW NOT--"
:GIGGLE:
THERE!
"--'WHEN I AM READY' CAME TO MEAN 'WHENEVER YOU WISH'!"
RAWA! RAWA!

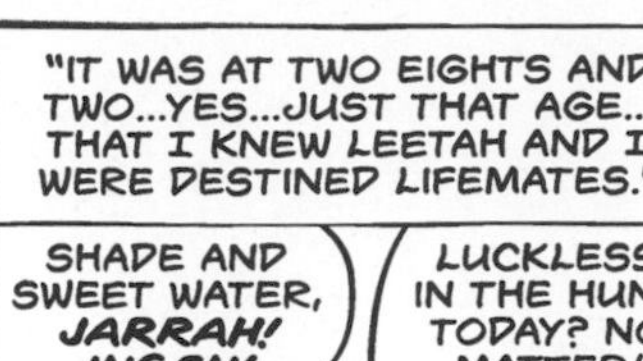
"IT WAS AT TWO EIGHTS AND TWO...YES...JUST THAT AGE... THAT I KNEW LEETAH AND I WERE DESTINED LIFEMATES."

SHADE AND SWEET WATER, JARRAH! INGEN!
LUCKLESS IN THE HUNT TODAY? NO MATTER! WHO NEEDS MEAT WHEN THERE'S BREAD APLENTY?!

HMPH! SPOKEN LIKE A TRUE DIRT DIGGER!
HA HA! DANCE, PRETTY LEETAH! DANCE THE GRAIN UP FROM THE GROUND!
ULP ULP

EH?

GASP

"LEETAH USED HER POWERS WITH NO MORE AWARENESS THAN IT TOOK TO DRAW BREATH.
"THAT WE TWO WERE UNIQUE ESCAPED HER. TO MY DISMAY, MANY THINGS SEEMED TO ESCAPE HER."
I TOLD YOU...THE JACKAL IS DEAD! I KILLED IT!

BUT...WHAT DOES IT MEAN... "DEAD"?
IT IS WHEN THE SPIRIT LEAVES THE BODY...AND NEVER COMES BACK.
ALL LIVING CREATURES CAN DIE...OR BE KILLED.

ALL...?
ALL!

SOME BEASTS, LIKE JACKALS, ARE WORTHLESS AND DESERVE TO DIE! OTHERS DO NOT DESERVE IT, BUT THEY DIE ANYWAY.

ELVES DON'T DIE!
THEY CAN--
--IF WE MAGIC-USERS FAIL TO LOOK AFTER THEM! I AM A HUNTER! YOU ARE A HEALER!

IT IS YOUR DUTY TO STUDY HARD WITH SAVAH, LIKE ME!
THE SUN FOLK WILL ALWAYS DEPEND ON THE TWO OF US... TOGETHER!

STUDY? DUTY? OH, RAYEK! WHAT AN OLD GLOOMER YOU ARE!
EVERYTHING IS FINE!

BUT MOTHER, WHY ARE THEY RUSHING TO HARVEST NOW?
"NO WARNINGS OF MINE COULD DISTURB HER CHILDISH BELIEF THAT ALL SHE KNEW--AND TOOK FOR GRANTED--WAS INVIOLATE.
"IT TOOK THE RUMBLE AND ROAR OF SMOKING MOUNTAIN--
"AND A RESULTING ZWOOT STAMPEDE--
"--TO TEACH THE PAMPERED KITLING THAT EVEN SHE MUST BOW TO THE WORLD'S UNFAIRNESS."
STAY HERE! IF WE TRY TO DRIVE THEM OUT, THEY WILL JUST CAUSE MORE DAMAGE!
BUT THEY'VE TRAMPLED THE GARDENS! THEY'RE EATING ALL THAT IS LEFT! DO SOMETHING!
"LEETAH HATED BEING AT THE MERCY OF CREATURES AND EVENTS MIGHTIER THAN HERSELF.
"YET THE WORLD KEPT ON FINDING WAYS TO DRIVE THAT VERY LESSON HOME!"
DO NOT FEAR THE DARK, CHILD. IT ALWAYS PASSES.
" 'THE DARK.' THE UTTER LOSS OF CONTROL, IN ANY SITUATION, BECAME HER GREATEST FEAR.

"IF MY EARLY YOUTH WAS HARD AS ROCK, LEETAH'S WAS SOFTENED WITH CUSHIONS AND SCENTED WITH OILS.
"WHEN SHE HAD REACHED TWO EIGHTS IN YEARS, SHE WAS MUCH IN DEMAND AS AN INITIATOR.' "

THIS NEW HUT IS NOT JUST FOR ME! ALL WILL BE WELCOME!
ALL INDEED! SHE IS MOST GENEROUS WITH HER SKILLS!
AND WE ARE MOST FORTUNATE!

"INITIATION..."

"SOMETIMES, RARELY, IT HEIGHTENS THE CHANCES OF RECOGNITION. FOR THAT REASON ONLY...COULD I BEAR LEETAH'S DELIGHT IN HER NEW ROLE."

:SSIIIGGHH: SWEET HEALER... SHOW US MORE!

I SHALL, ***THIRO***... AFTER A BREATH OF AIR!
AAAWW...!

OH! RAYEK! IT IS COLD OUT THERE!
WHY NOT COME SHARE WITH US?

SHARE?! I DO NOT BEGRUDGE YOU YOUR TASKS, LOVEMATE!
BUT YOU MUST SAVE SOMETHING... SOMETHING MOST SPECIAL...FOR ME!

"IF ANYONE WAS GENEROUS IN THOSE DAYS IT WAS I!
"BUT AT LAST I COULD NOT BEAR IT. LEETAH BELONGED TO ME!"

MY VEIL! BUT THERE IS NO WIND!
"IT WAS MY RIGHT TO CLAIM HER!"
AH, GOOD! THERE IT IS!
I SHOULD NOT LIKE TO LOSE IT!
!?!

OH...!
TEACH ME--

--WHAT YOU HAVE NEVER TAUGHT ME--
--OR ANYONE--BEFORE!

"SO SHE DID. I THOUGHT I MIGHT DIE FROM IT.

"BUT MORE...I HOPED TO LIVE!"
...R-RECOG... NITION...!
LET IT BE NOW...! I BEG YOU! NOW!

WHY?! WHY DO YOU HOLD BACK? I WANT ALL OF YOU!
YOU ARE MINE!

...N-NO...!

SO...IT IS TO BE A HUNT, THEN!

PANT PANT PANT
IF THAT IS WHAT RECOGNITION MUST COST ME--NO! NONE BUT I SHALL DECIDE WHEN...AND WITH WHOM!
"TIME PASSED. I WAS FORCED TO ACQUIRE SOMETHING AKIN TO PATIENCE.

"MY FRIVOLOUS LOVEMATE WAS BOUND TO COME TO HER SENSES--OF THAT I HAD NO DOUBT. SHE SIMPLY REQUIRED CONVINCING."
SHADE AND SWEET WATER, HEALER.
AND TO YOU THIS SPLENDID DAY, THIRO!

EH?!
AAAH...OF COURSE!

AND WHERE WOULD YOU LIKE THIS WATER TO GO, OH "HAIR OF SUNSET FIRE"?

BFGH!

:CHUCKLE: COME, THIRO!
A FINE WAY, INDEED, TO SAY FARE WELL!
FARE WELL...?

HE GOES TO THE CANYON AT THE BASE OF SMOKING MOUNTAIN. HE MEANS TO RETURN WITH TAME ZWOOTS OR NOT AT ALL!
HE ACTS FOR YOU, DAUGHTER! CAN YOU NOT WISH HIM WELL?
TAME ZWOOTS! OH, THE FOOL! THE GREAT BOASTFUL FOOL!

"MANY HARD, THIRSTY DAYS FOLLOWED. ONLY THE ANCIENT FOUNDERS HAD DARED SUCH A TREK--ON FOOT. TO SAY TRUTH, THE EFFORT FREED ME, AT TIMES, FROM THOUGHTS OF LEETAH.

"LATER I LEARNED SHE THOUGHT MUCH...AND OFTEN... OF ME!"

=GASP= FATHER! I SEE...A SPECK! MOVING AGAINST THE PALE SANDS!

"BY THE TIME I PASSED BENEATH THE GREAT ARCH OF THE ***BRIDGE OF DESTINY,*** *THE STARS WERE WELL ON THEIR WAY TO THEIR MORNING REST."*

COME CLOSER, SUN FOLK! NO NEED TO FEAR! THE BEASTS HAVE FELT MY POWER! THEY SLEEP AS THEY WALK!

FROM NOW ON THEY WILL BEAR YOUR HEAVY-LADEN BASKETS AND CLEAR AWAY FALLEN BOULDERS! THE ZWOOTS ARE YOURS TO COMMAND!

RAYEK! YOU DID IT!
OF COURSE! AS I HAVE ALWAYS SAID--
--WE MAGIC-USERS MUST TAKE CARE OF THE OTHERS. WHAT ARE THEY WITHOUT US?!
LOOK AT THE SIZE OF THIS ONE! HE IS AS TALL AS MY HUT!
=SNICKER= "HE" INDEED! WOULD THAT I WERE SO MAJESTICALLY FORMED!

"BASKING IN MY PEOPLE'S GRATITUDE, I FAILED TO NOTICE..."
SNUFF SNORT NYUUUHHH...?!
...MUSCLES ARE KNOTTED LIKE THE TRUNK OF A CLOUD-TREE, SEE? THINK OF THE WATER BAGS HE COULD CARRY--!
SNORRRT!
"THE LARGEST BEAST HAD SHRUGGED OFF MY SPELL."
UUNH!
THIRO! THIRO!
SOB SOB OH, THIRO...!
CARELESS OAF...! CHOKE I...I...
"IT WAS OVER IN AN INSTANT. LEETAH WAS POWERLESS. SHE COULD NOT BELIEVE IT."
THIS IS NOT YOUR FAULT, RAYEK! BUT IT IS WRONG! WRONG!
THIS...ENEMY... CAUGHT ME UNAWARES!
IT SHALL NOT DO SO AGAIN!

"WAILS OF MOURNING... THE FIRST I HAD EVER HEARD.. DRIFTED UP FROM THE VILLAGE INTO THE RECESSES OF MY CAVE.
"THIRO'S BLOOD WAS NOT ON MY HANDS--NOT TRULY. I HAD ONLY SOUGHT, AS ALWAYS, TO SERVE THE SUN FOLK WELL.
"BUT I WAS SORRY FOR THE POOR, DEAD ELF. AND I COULD NOT FORGET LEETAH'S VOW AS SHE HELD HIM."
EH...?! MY DAGGER! WHO TOOK--?
...NO!
OH, NO!
LEETAH?! WHERE ARE YOU?
LEETAH?!
...LEET--?
GASP

...

WHAT HAVE YOU DONE?!
I WILL FETCH HELP!

NO! L-LET ME BE!
I MUST... SEE...FOR MYSELF!
"MY FRIEND...MY DANCING, CARELESS FRIEND...SHIVERED WITHOUT A SOUND. WHERE HAD SHE FOUND SUCH COURAGE?
"BEFORE MY EYES, SHE WAS CHANGING...
"LEAVING ME BEHIND."
...DARK... THE DARK...IS COMING...
I... I CAN... ALMOST... SEE...!
≡GASP≡ IT IS HERE! I...KNOW... IT!
I SEE...ITS FACE...!

"WITH ONE FLASH OF A BLADE, LEETAH CAME MORE INTO HER OWN POWERS THAN ALL MY YEARS OF STUDY HAD EVER GAINED ME.

"SHARING THIRO'S JOURNEY, SHE HAD TAKEN HER OWN LIFE IN HER HANDS-- TO DEVOTE IT TO HER PEOPLE.

"THE ENEMY... THE DARKNESS WHICH OVERWHELMS, POSSESSES, ENGULFS THE LIGHT...WAS NO LONGER A FEARSOME STRANGER TO HER. SHE FACED IT--

"--AND CONQUERED! ALL WITHOUT SHOW, FOR NO ONE'S ACCLAIM! NONE BUT I WOULD KNOW."

IT--IT IS NOT ONLY DEATH... WHICH DEVOURS... RAYEK!
LOVE... CAN WEAR THE SAME MASK!

WHAT DO YOU MEAN?
NOTHING... I AM COLD... SO COLD!
"HER EYES WERE... OLDER.

"SHE THAT WAS MINE HAD FLOWN JUST BEYOND REACH... AND WOULD REMAIN SO.
"BUT I WOULD FOLLOW WITH HAND OUTSTRETCHED. I ALWAYS SHALL."
End

HYAAAAH HA HA HAAAH! I CANNOT FALL, WOLF CHIEF, BUT YOU MUST!
LEETAH IS BEYOND YOU!
N-NO...! THIS CAN'T BE...!
I'VE DONE THIS BEFORE! I-I CROSSED THE BRIDGE OF DESTINY... WON THE TRIAL OF HEAD, HAND, AND HEART...I KNOW I DID!
COME ON, CUTTER! DON'T SHAME US! DON'T SHAME LEETAH! GET UP!
...TOO HIGH...TOO HIGH...!
AAAH! THIS IS WHO YOU ARE, BLOOD OF TEN CHIEFS-- MORTAL! FULL OF MORTAL FEAR!

THE TRIAL IS OVER. WE TRUE ELVES WIN!
OUR CHILDREN SHALL BE HIGH ONES! NOTHING AWAITS YOU AND YOUR MONGREL TRIBE BUT--
--DEATH!
LEEETAAAHHH! DON'T! COME BAAAAACK!
SKYWISE! TREESTUMP! N-NIGHTFALL, PLEASE! STAY...! STAY! I-I'M--
FAAAALLLIIINNGG

:GASP:
OOOOHHH...
AGAIN, MY TAM?!
FROM YOUR WOLF BLOOD SPRINGS THE SAME DREAM, OVER AND OVER! IF I HAD THE POWER TO BLOT OUT THIS SELF-TORTURE--
--I WOULD! IS IT NOT ENOUGH THAT WE ARE TOGETHER AGAIN? WHAT WILL APPEASE THE WOUNDED BEAST INSIDE YOU? WHAT?!
LATER...
WONDER WHAT OLD RAYEK'S UP TO UNDER THE WAVES? BEEN PRETTY QUIET SINCE HIS LAST FLIGHT TO THE SUN VILLAGE?*
WHO KNOWS? THEY SAY IT'S SMART TO KEEP YOUR ENEMIES CLOSE--
*SEE HY #4--ED.
--BUT DEEP DOWN IN THE MUCK IS AS CLOSE AS I'LL EVER BE ABLE TO TOLERATE HIM!
YOU KNOW... YOU'LL HAVE TO GET ALONG WITH HIM SOMEHOW...IF YOU'RE EVER TO TRAVEL IN THE PALACE AGAIN.

HOW? FOR COUNTLESS EIGHTS MY FAMILY...YOU... WERE ALL DEAD TO ME-- BECAUSE OF HIM!
I TRY TO LIVE IN THE "NOW"--
--BUT IT CHEWS MY GUT--
"--TO KNOW HE'S DOWN THERE, STILL CONTENT WITH HIMSELF, STILL FOOLING WITH POWERS THAT CAN CHANGE EVERYONE'S WORLD--EVERYONE'S LIFE--BUT HIS!"
BE STILL... ALL OF YOU! IT...IS...THE LAD!
?!
WHAT WAS THAT, BROWN-SKIN?
EKUAR, HUSH! SUNTOP SENDS AGAIN, FROM BEYOND THE VASTDEEP WATER!

NOW, WHAT IS THIS YOU SHOW ME, YOUNG GUIDE? STRANGE...! BEAUTIFUL...!
THE VISION CAME WITH THE OPEN SENDING, RAYEK.
FROM WHOM?
HE SENT ONLY ONCE. I'M NOT SURE...BUT IT FEELS LIKE HE'S SOMEWHERE... FAR BELOW SORROW'S END...BELOW THE DESERT! IS THAT POSSIBLE?
THERE IS BUT ONE WAY TO LEARN! WE MUST INVESTIGA--
--EH?!
SUDDEN RAGE... AND THE TENUOUS CONTACT IS BROKEN.
WILL THE WOLF CHIEF NEVER RELENT?! SUNTOP SAYS HE IS FORBIDDEN TO FLY WITH ME EVER AGAIN UNLESS CUTTER GOES TOO!
=SIGH= THAT WON'T HAPPEN ANYTIME SOON, I FEAR.

I KNOW, ZHANTEE... AND I KNOW WHY!
BUT EVEN SO--
--THE PALACE OF THE HIGH ONES SHOULD ALWAYS BE FREE, FOR ALL ELVES' USE! IF I CAN LEARN SUCH A LESSON--
--THEN CUTTER TOO MUST LEARN THAT HE CAN TRUST ME TO BRING HIM AND HIS OWN SAFELY HOME, FROM ANY JOURNEY!
I MUST ACT ON SUNTOP'S NEWS!
WHAT WILL FREE ME FROM CUTTER'S HATRED? WHAT WILL IT TAKE, VENKA?
TELL ME!
HE NEEDS TO FORGET...
...EVEN AS A WOLF FORGETS WHEN A CHALLENGE IS FOUGHT AND DONE.
SO...IT IS A FIGHT HE NEEDS! FINE!
I CAN GIVE HIM THAT, AND WELCOME!
YOU HAVEN'T TRULY FACED HIM SINCE YOU TOOK HIS FAMILY AWAY.
HE HAS... CHANGED!

SO HAVE I! HE HAS HIS KIN CLOSE TO HIM AGAIN. BUT ONE I LOVE--
--STILL SLEEPS BEYOND MY EMBRACE.

THE LONG YEARS OF YEARNING...! NO MATTER THE DIFFERENCE IN DEGREE, I TOO KNOW THAT SADNESS.
AND UPON THAT GROUND THE WOLFRIDER AND I MEET AS EQUALS!
THAT IS NOT WHAT I MEANT, FATHER. HE--

--WILL BE UNABLE TO *RESIST* MY CHALLENGE! TAKE IT TO HIM *QUICKLY,* DAUGHT--
--ER...I MEAN... PLEASE! THE SOONER WE CLEAR THE AIR, THE SOONER WE SHALL BE SOARING THROUGH IT!

*UNAWARE OF EVENTS TAKING SHAPE, THE WOLFRIDER ELDERS HOLD SECRET COUNSEL WITHIN **TREESTUMP** AND **CLEARBROOK'S** DEN...*

WE MEET THIS DAY TO DIG UP A CACHE OF MEMORIES THE YOUNGER ONES DON'T SHARE.

AYE! HERE IT IS: CUTTER'S OUR CHIEF AND MY CLOSE BLOOD KIN. ANYONE KNOWS ME KNOWS I'LL DOUBLE-KNOT THE FIRST TONGUE THAT WAGS AGAINST HIM!

UNDER HIS RULE WE'VE HAD A STRETCH OF PEACE AND QUIET LIKE NONE WE OLD GROWLERS CAN RECALL. BUT--

--BUT WOULD WE BE GATHERING THUS IF ALL WAS TRULY WELL...?

AS EVER, STRONGBOW'S HIT THE MARK! ALL THESE SEASONS IN ONE HOLT...ONE TERRITORY...
...WITH NO RECOGNITIONS-- AND ONLY OUR SWEET TYLEET MAKING IT FROM CUB TO FULL GROWTH!
SOMEHOW, IT GOES AGAINST "THE WAY."
"THERE USED TO BE DEATHS.
"AND TERRIBLE BATTLES.
"AND NEW LIVES TO REPLACE THOSE LOST. OR AM I SEEING THROUGH A DREAM MIST?"
YOU SEE CLEARLY, TREESTUMP.
IT IS STAGNATION'S APPROACH YOU FEAR--
--AND RIGHTLY SO! FOR IT CAN BE DEADLY, AS THE GLIDERS LEARNED...TO THEIR SORROW!
BUT HOW DO WE TELL CUTTER WE MUST ALLOW DANGER AND DEATH BACK INTO THE--
RRAAAAUGGH!
--HOLT...?!

AAARRGGGGGHHHHHH!
OOOOOO!
KRAK

HEY, CUTTER!
"IN THE TREES AS YOU PLEASE, ON THE GROUND NOT A SOUND," REMEMBER...? YUK YUK

RRR-RRR-RRR...

KPOW
NICELY DONE, SKOT!

HMPH! SOME SHOW! SO THAT HOME-WRECKING RAYEK'S SPOILING FOR A FIGHT, IS HE?
YES, PICKNOSE! VENKA DELIVERED HIS CHALLENGE MOMENTS AGO. BUT THERE IS MORE TO IT THAN--
--WHAT GALL! WHAT ARROGANCE!

I LIKE IT! SEND THE FLEABAG AND THE MAGIC SPOUTER DOWN TO MY REALM!
THEY'LL SUPPLY THE FLYING FUR AND TEETH--WE TROLLS WILL PROVIDE AN ARENA FIT FOR SUCH A SPECTACLE!

COME, TRINKET, MY JEWEL! GOOD THING YOU RAN AWAY THIS TIME--
--OR WE'D HAVE MISSED THE CHANCE TO SEE THAT CHILD SNATCHER GET HIS UGLY POINTED EARS HAMMERED BACK!

IS IT TO BE... BELOVED?
PANT PANT PANT
IT IS!
COME!
COME!
COME!
HE ACCEPTS.
WISH ME WELL, WINNOWILL.
SOON...
HEH HEH, HURRY UP, LITTLE BUG-EYES, THEY'RE WAITING!
THIS WAY-- TO GET YOUR BUTT POUNDED INTO HASH, BABY STEALER!
OH... MY...!

EEEHEEE EEEHEEE!
EEEHEE EEEHEEE!
YEEK! YEEK!
HOO HOO! HOO I'D SCOOT RIGHT ON BACK TO THE BIG PUDDLE IF I WERE YOU, SHIVER-SHANKS!
HE CAME, PAPA! THE BAD ELF CAME!

I BET MY BEST PAIR OF TONGS THE WOLF-ELF'LL CRY "MERCY" FIRST, BLACK-HAIR! DON'T LET ME DOWN!
NYAAHH! "BUTTERFLY-LEGS," THERE, WON'T STAND UP TO ONE PUNCH!
K-KK-KK-CH!

THE WOLFRIDERS... EVEN THEIR WOLVES ARE HERE--

"--BUT WHERE IS...?"

SILENCE! YOUR PATRIARCH SPEAKS! BY MY MAGNANIMOUS CONSENT THE LOWLY ELVES ARE HERE ALLOWED TO RESOLVE, HAND TO HAND, AN ANCIENT GRUDGE!
THERE ARE JUST THREE RULES--
--ONE: NO MAGIC! ALL ELSE IS FAIR!
TOO SCAT-SCARED TO RISK YOUR HIDE AVENGING YOUR OWN WHELP, EH, PICKY?

TWO: NO DYING TO SAVE FACE! BOTH MUST SURVIVE!

THREE: HE THAT FIRST CALLS FOR HEALING--LOSES! AND ONE MUST CALL!

SO...ALL THINGS COME FULL CIRCLE!
LITTLE MORE THAN TWO EIGHTS AGO I DUELED THE WOLFRIDER FOR WOOING RIGHTS TO LEETAH--AND WAS SURPRISED BY DEFEAT IN THE TRIAL OF HAND!
BUT VENKA HAS HELPED ME BUILD GREAT BODY STRENGTH OF LATE. AND CUTTER IS STILL, AFTER ALL--
"--A MERE YOUTH!"
!!!
HEH HEH HEH HEH...
SNARF SNARF
HNNH HNNH HNNH...THIS IS GONNA BE GOOD!

SCORNING PICKNOSE'S SIGNAL TO BEGIN, THE OPPONENTS EYE EACH OTHER.
WHAT WILL TRIGGER THE FIRST BLOW?
HHHHHUUUUUNNNNNHHHH!

EEAAAGHH!
UNH!
UUFF!
WELL DONE, CUTTER! BUT YOU SPOILED THE ROAST! HAR HAR!
YAAAAHHH--!

--AAAAAHHH!

HHOOOOFF!

LOOK OUT!

WATCH IT!

UUNH!

CATCH 'IM!

OOO! PICKY! HELP!
HUUNH!
GASP
THUD
SMASH 'IM ONE, BLACK-HAIR!
BUT NOT HERE! PI-I-I-ICKY! DO SOME-THING!
CUTTER!
HEY! GET BACK IN THE ARENA, YOU ROTTEN LITTLE--
I'LL FIX 'EM!
YEAH! SHOVE 'EM OFF!

YAAH!
GASP CHOKE
HEY! THAT'S CHEATING!
...FALLING...!
GRRRR-RRRR...!
...FORGOT... FOR A MOMENT...!
GO GET 'IM, FLEA-FEAST!
OOOFF!
UUNNNHH!
BOK
NNNGH!
HEY! OL' BUTTERFLY'S SNEAKING OUT!
...NEED... TIME...!
COUGH COUGH
CATCH HIM, CUTTER! COME ON!

DON'T WANNA MISS THIS!
OUT THAT ARCHWAY! HURRY!
SMICKETY-SMACK! SMICKETY-SMACK!
BUSYHEAD HIGHTHING AND SHARPDARK HIGHTHING GO TUMBLE-RUMBLE!

IT'S NO USE! I CAN HEAR YOU...

...SMELL YOU...

...TRACK YOU...

...ANYWHERE YOU--

--RUN...?!

--OR CLIMB?
HAAAAH!
URRRRGH!
UNH!
AAGH!
HNNH!
UUHH!

GO AHEAD! BITE IT OFF, CUTTER! I'LL FIX IT LATER-- MAYBE!
OO OOOO OOO! BET THAT HURT!
QUIT PIDDLE-DIDDLING AND DO SOME REAL DAMAGE, WOLF-ELF! I'VE GOT FOUR BAGS OF "FIRE-EYES" WAGED ON YOU!
THAT'S NOT WHAT THIS IS FOR!
WHAT ELSE?! THE WIN'S ALREADY POURED AND SET!
THE FUN'S IN SEEING HOW MUCH THE CHILD-THIEF CAN TAKE!
AAANH!
NOW THAT'S MORE LIKE IT!
YESSS! GO FOR THE KILL!

STAND STRONG, FATHER! NOT ALL ARE AGAINST YOU!
UUNNHHH!
KLOPP
PANT... PANT... PANT.
PANT COUGH

·GASP· CU--
UUUFF!
CHAK
FROM BEHIND! WHY, THAT--
NO, LOVEMATE! ALL BUT MAGIC IS FAIR!
GET DOWN HERE!
GLADLY!
YOU WANT "DOWN," MUMPLINGS?
HAPPY TO OBLIGE!
HAAAWWW HAAAW HAW HAW--
KRASH

--HAW-W-W-WAAAAAAH!
DUNG CHIP!
GAAAK PTOOTH!
BLOAT-BELLIED SAND SLUG!
OH, PUCKERNUTS! MENDER!
WOODLOCK AND RAINSONG'S "GENTLE" CUB, EH?
ONLY ONE FIGHT COUNTS HERE! JUST COOL OFF TILL YOU'RE NEEDED--!
"--AND THAT'LL BE SOON ENOUGH!"
OOOOWWWW!

UNH-SSSSS...!
HUNH?!
YOU'D BETTER CALL. HURTING YOU DOESN'T BOTHER ME.
EEEE-YUUUH!
KTUNG
NNNGHH!
NOW...!

FEEL THAT...? HOTTER THAN THE DESERT, EH?
GASP
CALL!
N-N...
NO...?
SSS-S-KSSSHHH
EEEEYAAAAAAHHHH!
Y-YOU WERE... NEVER...LIKE THIS...!
...NEVER... CRUEL!
YOU KILLED MY FAMILY!
FOR EIGHT EIGHTS TIMES EIGHT I WAITED FOR THEM--!
--AND THAT KILLED ME!

LOOK! I'LL SHOW YOU...WHAT I'LL SHOW NO ONE ELSE!
SEE? THAT'S PEACE...! PAST LOVE...PAST WANT... PAST THINKING TO TAKE ANOTHER BREATH!
THE WORLD COULD CHANGE ITSELF CRAZY ALL AROUND ME...BUT WITH THEM I HAD THE "NOW"!
WOLFRIDERS DON'T USE WORDS FOR WHAT THEY HAVE...ONLY FOR WHAT THEY DON'T HAVE!
YOU TAUGHT ME WORDS FOR MY FAMILY...FOR THE "NOW OF WOLF-THOUGHT"... AND FOR PEACE!
AND NOW I CAN'T FORGET... CAN'T STOP FEELING TIME PASS...! CAN'T STOP COUNTING...!

YOU MADE
ME HUMAN!

NOW DO YOU SEE? DO YOU?
NO...! NOOOO!
TAKE YOUR PAIN FROM MY HEAD! I DON'T WANT TO SEE--!
--DON'T WANT TO KNOW!
THAT'S YOUR PROBLEM!
BOKK
!!!
?!
CALL...! CALL!
...NO!

I HEARD THAT! THAT WAS A RIB-- AND MORE!
END IT! CALL NOW!

COUGH
NO...!

...YOU HAVEN'T...HAD... ENOUGH!

WHAT?! YOU'RE CRAZY! I ALWAYS KNEW IT!
TWIG-WALKING, BEAR-POKING--

--CRAZY!
KT-KT
KT-KT KTAKK
PANT...PANT... WHEEZE...PANT... PANT...
UUUUNNNHH... UUH-GUH...!

COUGH COUGH
COME ON... PANT PANT... IT'S OVER...!
CALL!
AAAAGH!
NO!
YOU HAVEN'T GASP HAD--
--ENOUGH!
THUD
AAAIIEEEE!

H-HIGH ONES...!
BOTH OF THEM...! BOTH!
CAN YOU WATCH THIS ANY LONGER, LEETAH?
?!
THERE ARE DIFFERENT KINDS OF HEALING.
GASP WHEEZE
STUBBORN FOOL! YOU CAN'T DIE! BUT...I'LL-MAKE-YOU-SEE-DEATH-COMING!
CALL, CURSE YOU! CALL!
N-NOT... SKK... NOT 'TIL... YOU'VE HAD... ENOUGH!
UNBELIEVABLE!
HOO HOO HEEE! NOW THAT'S ONE HIGH-NOSED ELF!
STILL THINKS HE'S WINNING! HA HA! WHAT A ROCK-SKULL!

RRR- ***RRR***-RRRRR... GRRRR...!

GH... ...

..."'TIL YOU'VE HAD ENOUGH...?!"
=GASP= NOT TO CUTTER--!

--FOR CUTTER!

HE IS DOING IT FOR CUTTER!
!
?
?!

THANK YOU...FOR RAISING...MY DAUGHTER...!

LEETAH...

LEETAH...?
HERE... ALWAYS!

COUGH COUGH
EASY... MY CHIEF!

RAAAZZZZZ
IS HE--?
HE'S FINE, NIGHTFALL. NEVER BETTER!
CUTTER! YOU TWIT! YOU NINNY!
BOTCHED A ROMANCE! NOW HE BOTCHES REVENGE...!

SHHHH! I WILL SOFTEN THE GROUND!

YOU DO KNOW HOW TO LOVE AFTER ALL!

WORTHLESS, WASP-WAISTED, FEEBLE...COST ME FOUR BAGS OF...AND AFTER ALL I BLAH BLAH BLAH...
CUTTER... WHO WON?
...YOU KNOW.
The End

IT IS ONLY AN EIGHT OF DAYS SINCE CUTTER AND HIS TRIBE AWOKE FROM THEIR TEN THOUSAND YEAR HIBERNATION. IN THIS STRANGE LAND, THEY CAREFULLY, HOPEFULLY BREATHE LIFE INTO THE HEART OF A NEW HOLT ON THORNY MOUNTAIN.
THAT'S BETTER, MOONSHADE. NOW LEETAH CAN GET AROUND IN THE WOODS.
THOUGH YOU HATE THE DRESS, BELOVED, THE COLOR SUITS ME, DON'T YOU THINK?
ALL THE REST OF THIS CLOTH WILL KEEP YOU IN MENDS 'TIL CUTTER'S FACE FUR IS DOWN TO HIS KNEES, HEALER!
DREAMTIME
I STILL CAN'T BELIEVE THE HUMANS MADE THIS. IT'S SO SOFT AND FINE... LIKE A DREAM.

"LIKE A DREAM..."
YOU SHOULD BE SCARFING DREAMBERRIES, TREE-SHAPER! BUT SOMETHING'S BEEN EATING YOU SINCE WE WOKE UP! ULP ULP WHAT GIVES?
I'M TRYING TO REMEMBER. I KNOW WE SLEPT...

...AND I HAVE THE FEELING WE DREAMED. BUT I CAN'T RECALL ANYTHING. I GUESS IT'S NOT IMPORTANT.

UURRP NOW THAT'S WHERE YOU'RE WRONG! I HAPPEN TO THINK DREAMS ARE VERY IMPORTANT!
THEY CAN TEACH YOU VALUABLE STUFF.

JUST 'CAUSE YOU CAN'T REMEMBER DOESN'T MEAN YOU SHOULDN'T, REDLANCE. ALL YOUR HEAD NEEDS IS A JOG SIDEWAYS!
NOW, IN MY DEN, I HAPPEN TO HAVE A FULL SKIN OF OLD MAGGOTY'S CHOICEST DREAMBERRY BREW. YOU JUST COME WITH ME, AND...

LATER...
WHEW! POTENT! YOU KNOW HIC I DON'T NORMALLY LIKE TO ADDLE MY SENSES THIS MUCH.
SURE. SURE. BUT YOU CAN'T REMEMBER DEEP-BURIED DREAMS WHEN THE WORLD'S TOO MUCH WITH YOU.
"JUST RELAX, LIKE ME. LET YOUR MIND WANDER...

"...TO THE BANKS OF THE DREAM RIVER. STOP THERE. ASK FOR WHAT'S PAST TO FLOAT BY AGAIN."
MMMM... PERCHED ON THE EDGE... BETWEEN WAKING AND SLEEPING...
"I SEE... AAAH! NOW I REMEMBER...!
"I AM THE SPIRIT OF THE FATHER TREE... IN THE HOLT WHERE WE WERE BORN! MY BODY IS OLD BEYOND TELLING. BARK AND BRANCH, LEAF AND DEEP BURIED ROOT DRAW THEIR LIFE FROM THE SOIL, AND FROM EVERY LIVING THING AROUND THEM!
"I GIVE BREATH TO ALL CREATURES DWELLING NEAR ME AND IN ME. I AM CONNECTED TO MANY OTHERS SUCH AS I! IN THE FOREST, WHAT ONE FEELS, ALL FEEL.
"THE KNOWING IS DEEP AND UNQUESTIONING --LIKE A LOCK-SEND THAT NEVER ENDS. THERE IS NO LONELINESS, NO SUCH THING AS SEPARATION.

"LOOK! AS THEY HAVE DONE FOR GENERATIONS, WOLFRIDERS RACE AWAY FROM THE HOLT ON THEIR NIGHTLY HUNT! I WISH THEM WELL AS THEY GO TO KEEP THE FOREST'S LIVING THINGS IN BALANCE.
"SPIRITS FILL ME FROM ROOTS TO TOP LEAVES! ALL THOSE WHO HAVE DWELT WITHIN ME -- THEY ARE WITH ME STILL!
"EVEN BEYOND DEATH GOODTREE, MY SHAPER, LENDS HER POWERS SO MY BODY CONTINUES TO GROW IN FORMS THAT MEAN 'HOME' TO THE ELVES.

"AS THE YEARS PASS IN THEIR MANY EIGHTS-OF-EIGHT, SEASONS CHANGING IN ENDLESS CYCLES, LIVING TREE-SHAPERS WORK WITH THE SPIRITS TO KEEP ME AND MY BRETHREN HEALTHY AND STRONG.
"THIS IS WHAT IT IS TO BE TRULY IMMORTAL, FOR EVEN THE WHITE COLD MEANS NOT DEATH, ONLY SLEEP...
"...AND NOT SOLELY FOR ME AND MY FELLOW TREES, BUT FOR THOSE WHO REST INSIDE ME, SAFE AND WARM, AWAITING THE TIME OF NEW GREEN.
"LOVE FOR THESE 'SEEDLINGS' OF MINE COURSES THROUGH MY LIMBS EVEN AS THE SAP THEY CALL BLOOD PULSES THROUGH THEIR VEINS.
"BUT THEN... ONE DAY... SPARKS! SPARKS OF FIRE BORNE ON THE WIND! THEY TOUCH MY LEAVES, CLING TO MY BARK -- AND BURN!
"MY BROTHERS AT THE FOREST'S EDGE CRY OUT: HUMANS! THE ONE CALLED SPIRIT MAN AND HIS FOLLOWERS! THEY HAVE DONE THIS!
"POOR SOULS! DON'T THEY KNOW? THEIR DEED OF FEAR AND VENGEANCE AGAINST THE ELVES WILL CONSUME THEM AS WELL!"

"THE WOLFRIDERS FLEE. AND WELL THEY SHOULD, FOR THERE IS NOTHING THEY CAN DO.
"I FEEL THE DEADLY HEAT, AS DO MY FELLOW TREES! SEARING AGONY! WE SCREAM WITH ONE VOICE.
"YET, THERE IS NO FEAR... EVEN NOW. FOR JUST AS WOLVES THIN THE DEER HERDS, MAKING THEM STRONGER, SO THE FLAMES THIN THE FOREST.
"THIS BLAZE MIGHT HAVE BEEN CAUSED BY AN UNEXPECTED BOLT OF SKYFIRE. THERE IS NO RESENTMENT IN ME. IT IS MY TIME.
"IT GOES ON LONG... **LONG**... THE BURNING! AT LAST, THE FLAMES BEGIN TO DIE...
"...FEEL MYSELF... CRUMBLING TO AN ASHEN STUMP...
"...LIFE FORCE... ALL BUT DRAINED... FROM ME AND MY BRETHEN...!
"...SPIRITS OF ALL TREE-SHAPERS... HELP US...!

"DOWN BENEATH THE SCORCHED FOREST FLOOR, DOWN WHERE THE SOIL IS STILL MOIST AND RICH, I AM CALLED TO A *HEALING*.

"OH, SEE! OUR *ROOTS*! OUR ROOTS HAVEN'T BEEN DESTROYED! I KNOW NOW, MY BRETHREN AND I WILL GROW BACK! IT WILL TAKE MANY, MANY EIGHTS OF SEASONS, A LONG, SLOW, UPWARD CLIMB TO THE LIGHT."

BUT, SOMEDAY, ALL SHALL BE AS IT WAS. THE WOLFRIDERS, THE CHILDREN BORN IN MY WOODEN WOMB, WILL RETURN TO ME.

SNIFFLE BEAUTIFUL! WHAT A BEAUTIFUL DREAM!

I HOPE WE *CAN* GO HOME TO OUR BIRTH-HOLT AND SEE THE FATHER TREE REGROWN!

TREES ARE LIKE HIGH ONES, I GUESS. *SNIFF* THEY LIVE FOREVER!

SOMETHING... SOMETHING *ELSE* IS COMING...!

"THE HOLT IS DESERTED. THE WOLFRIDERS WERE HERE, BUT THEY HAVE GONE AGAIN.
"A NEW THREAT APPROACHES...
"HUMANS! HUMANS COME AT ME AND MY BRETHREN WITH WEAPONS OF METAL! THE ONE THING THAT CAN DESTROY US UTTERLY!
"TERRIBLE, LONG, SHARP-TOOTHED BLADES...!
"NOW THERE IS PAIN, RESENTMENT AND FEAR, FOR THE METAL BLADES ARE MAN-MADE AND WITH DARK INTENT...
"...AND THE HUMANS WILL NOT STOP 'TIL THE DESTRUCTION IS COMPLETE!

"OOOHHH... I'M BLEEDING...! CUT IN TWO!
"HAVE PITY, YOU MEN OF DAYS TO COME!
"NOW I TRULY DIE, MY HEART-ROOT RIPPED OUT BY A SMOKE-BELCHING, METAL BEAST LIKE NONE THE FOREST HAS EVER SEEN!
"WOLFRIDERS! LOVING SPIRITS! FARE WELL! I DIE FOREVER!
AAAAH!!
REDLANCE! IT'S ME! YOU'RE SAFE! COME ON, WAKE UP!
HUH?! WHA--?!

REDLANCE! WHAT'S WRONG?
NOTHING, CUTTER! JUST A BAD DREAM!
BELOVED, ARE YOU ALL RIGHT?

I'VE NEVER HEARD YOU CRY OUT SO!
I'VE NEVER SEEN -- OR FELT -- THE THINGS I DID THIS EVENING.
QUICKLY, REDLANCE AND PIKE EXPLAIN ...

GETTING TORN OUT BY THE ROOTS... ***THAT'S*** WHAT I'LL NEVER FORGET. IS IT A SYMBOL, PIKE, OR A WARNING?

MAYBE BOTH! THE DREAM'S UNFINISHED. THERE'S A TEACHING IN IT THAT NEEDS UNCOVERING.

YOU SAID, WITH TREES, WHAT ONE FEELS, ALL FEEL. MAYBE, WITH US, WHAT ONE DREAMS, ***ALL*** DREAM.

IF SO, BELOVED, ***ALL*** WHO SLEPT SHOULD TRY TO REMEMBER. THE ***SHARED*** WISDOM OF THE DREAMS COULD BE VITAL.

HMM... COULD BE! SO WHO'S NEXT?

I AM!

NEWS OF REDLANCE'S DISTURBING DREAM GATHERS CURIOUS MEMBERS OF THE WOLFRIDER TRIBE IN THE HEART OF THORNY MOUNTAIN HOLT.
SPURRED BY THE VISION'S RETELLING, OTHERS LOOK DEEP -- INTO SHADOW PLACES WITHIN THEIR MINDS TO SEE IF CONNECTING IMAGES EMERGE.
WELL, PIKE, THIS IS YOUR SQUIRRELLY GAME. WHOSE NIGHTMARE GETS COUGHED UP NEXT?
IT'S GOOD TO LOOK FOR SOME MEANING... AFTER OUR LONG SLEEP UNDERGROUND. I'LL TRY --
--UH UH, NIGHTFALL! SEEMS TO ME THE ONE WHO WAS IN REDLANCE'S DREAM SHOULD GO NEXT.
DREAMTIME Pt. 2
HUH? THE ONE IN HIS DREAM?
TREE SPIRITS...? DEAD ELF SPIRITS...?
AW C'MON...! HUMANS?!

HEH HEH, NO, SKOT. DREAMS SOMETIMES PLAY WITH NAMES... TURN THEM INTO PICTURES.
REDLANCE SAW BURNT TREESTUMPS IN HIS DREAM!
IT'S TRUE! HE DID!
WELL, HANG ME RUMP SKYWARD!
SIGH AWFUL WEIRD, PIKE! SO...?
SO-O-O...
"...WE SEND FOR TREESTUMP, ROCK-BRAIN!"
COCOONED TOGETHER FOR A MOUNTAIN'S AGE, OLD FRIEND, BUT I GUESS WE'RE BOTH STILL PRETTY SHARP! HEH HEH HEH...
DA DUMMM... DA DUMMM... DA DA DA FILLS THE NIGHT... FRIENDLY DARKNESS, WINKING ST--
WHURF!
KSHHIK
KSHHIK
KSHHIK
TREESTUMP!
TREESTUMP!
A COUNCIL!
HUH?!
COMING!

MY DREAMS...?! OWL PELLETS! YOU HAULED MY TAIL HERE FOR THAT?!
CAN'T RECALL A CURSED THING--AND THAT'S JUST FINE WITH ME!
BUT--BUT THINK OF THE STORIES I COULD TELL!
COME ON! JUST TRY SOME DREAM-BERRIES--
--TO JOG YOUR MEMORY-- URRK!
AND ARE YOU THE ONE TO SHOVE 'EM DOWN MY GULLET IF I SAY NO?
UMM... UH... W-WELL...
HEH HEH... DREAMBERRIES WORKED FOR REDLANCE 'CAUSE HE'S FULL OF PLANT MAGIC.
M-MAYBE SOMETHING ELSE WILL SPARK YOUR--
--THE ONLY SPARKS YOU'LL SEE, MEDDLER, I'LL BE MAKING WITH MY SHARPSTONE!
UFF!
WHICH IS WHAT I WAS DOING WHEN YOU INTERRUPTED ME!
GRUMBLE ... GROWL ... RRRRR
I'M WITH TREESTUMP, BELOVED. FINDING THE COMMON MESSAGE IN A BUNCH OF SLEEP-PICTURES--
--SEEMS AS SILLY AS TRYING TO PIN RAINDROPS TOGETHER WITH AN ARROW.
HMMM...

THERE MAY BE MORE TO TREE-STUMP'S REFUSAL THAN HE LETS ON.
I'LL GO FIND OUT.

DON'T GO FAR!
NEVER... NEVER AGAIN, BELOVED!

PIKE'S RIGHT! DREAMS ARE IMPORTANT, MOTHER. ANYWAY, I THINK SO!
MAYBE YOU CAN CONVINCE TREESTUMP OF THAT, MY LITTLE SUNTOP!

AND...
IS IT THAT YOU DON'T WANT TO REMEMBER, OLD FRIEND?
OH, LASS, IT WAS SO SAD WITHOUT YOU AND THE TWINS.
NOW WE'RE ALL TOGETHER AGAIN. WHY NOT JUST LIVE IN THE "NOW"?
KSHHIK
KSHHIK

HEY! YOU DO REMEMBER SOMETHING!
PLEASE... TELL US.

KA-SHHIK! KA-SHHIK!
METAL...
"NO ELF HOLDS THE SECRET OF ITS MAKING. THAT'S FOR TROLLS TO KNOW...
"...OR IT WAS!"

"REDLANCE DREAMT OUR BIRTH-HOLT WILL BE DESTROYED BY HUMANS... WITH GREAT BLADES MADE ALL OF METAL!
"METAL WEAPONS IN HUMAN HANDS! TERRIBLE! BUT I -- I THINK I'VE SEEN EVEN WORSE.
"IN MY DREAM, I SEE MYSELF... AT LEAST THE GUARDIAN SPIRIT I THINK IS ME... BIG AS LIFE... NO, BIGGER... WIELDING AND WEARING THE SHINY STUFF.
"I BORROW ITS PROTECTIVE POWER... BECOME PART OF ITS MYSTERY.

"THE MYSTERY BEGINS WITH FIRE, THAT MUCH I KNOW. FROM GROUND TO MELTING POT... THEN TO COOL AIR AND HAMMER BLOWS.
"ALL THE MAKINGS OF THE WORLD ITSELF GO INTO THE FORGING OF A BLADE!
"IT BEGINS IN FIRE AND FINISHES IN WATER. BUT THE BLADE ONLY LIVES -- REALLY LIVES -- WHEN MY HAND GRASPS IT!

"HOW DO I USE THE SHARP, SHINING GIFT? I SERVE!
"CUBS AND KIN... LIFEMATES AND CHIEFS... I GET BETWEEN THEM AND ALL THE DANGERS THERE ARE TO FACE.
"IT MAKES ME GLAD. IT'S ALL I WANT.

"TO FEED!
"TO PROTECT!

"AND I LOVE IT!
"NOTHING CAN WITHSTAND THE KEEN EDGES OF MY TWO BLADES, THE STRENGTH IN MY TWO GOOD ARMS!
"WHEN I SEE BLOOD FLOW, I THIRST FOR MORE!
RRRAAAUUGH!!
"AND THERE IS ALWAYS MORE!

"I'M AS STRONG AS MY SWORD... AS MIGHTY AS MY AXE... AS UNHURTABLE AS MY ARMOR!"
HA HA HA HA HA HA HA
HEYYOOOO!!!
"I SWING MY BLADES IN TRIUMPH, SLASHING THE AIR. THOSE I LOVE AND PROTECT HOWL FOR JOY!"
AYOOOAH!!
AYYOOOAH!!
"NO FORCE CAN FELL ME --

"--UNTIL... OH, HIGH ONES! THE TREES... THE TREES CLOSE IN!
"THE FOREST SHRINKS! NO ROOM FOR SLASHING!
"BUT MY AXE! MY SWORD-- THEY SWING OUT OF CONTROL! HIGH ONES! CAN'T STOP!
"WATCH OUT, CUBS! WATCH OUT!
"CUBS!

"NO...!
"OH, NO.......

"THE WORLD'S GIFT, OUT OF CONTROL, HAS TAKEN MY DEAR ONES AWAY!
"TEARS...
"NOTHING COULD STOP THOSE COLD, SCREAMING BLADES.
"BUT MY TEARS WEAR THEM DOWN... TO NOTHING!
"SO IT FINISHES IN WATER... A GREAT WAVE OF SALT TEARS... OVERWHELMING ALL!"

...THAT'S ALL I REMEMBER. AND I'LL NOT TELL IT AGAIN.
WE... UNDERSTAND.
WE'LL TELL IT FOR YOU, TREESTUMP. ANYWAY, I BET YOU HAD BETTER, HAPPIER DREAMS THAN THAT.
TRY TO REMEMBER THOSE.
AYE, CUB, BUT THIS IS THE ONE THAT STICKS. MAYBE PIKE CAN MAKE SOMETHING OF IT.
I'M JUST NOT SURE I WANT TO KNOW.
AND WHEN LEETAH HAS FAITHFULLY REPORTED TREESTUMP'S NIGHTMARE...
AFTER ALL WE'VE BEEN THROUGH, WHY HAUNT OURSELVES WITH DARK MIND-STUFF THAT SHOULD STAY BURIED?
BELOVED, WE MUST CONTINUE!
UM... CUTTER. I -- I DON'T MEAN TO SPEAK OUT OF TURN, BUT...
TREESTUMP'S DREAM... IT REMINDS ME. I'VE DREAMT OF BIG WAVES LIKE THAT SINCE I WAS A CHILD.
DID YOU SEE ONE WHILE WE SLEPT UNDERGROUND, ZHANTEE?
THAT... AND MORE. I'D LIKE TO TELL EVERYONE...
...IF IT'S ALL RIGHT, CUTTER...

TWO OF THE ELFIN TRIBE -- REDLANCE AND TREESTUMP -- HAVE TOLD OF THEIR NIGHTMARES, AND NOW PIKE'S DREAM-TEACHING GAME TAKES A DISTURBING TURN --
-- ESPECIALLY FOR THE WOLFRIDERS' QUICK-TEMPERED CHIEF.
CUTTER...? IS IT ALL RIGHT IF I GO NEXT?
WHAT FOR, ZHANTEE? WE'VE A NEW HOLT TO SETTLE AND GAME TO HUNT --
-- AND FOR THAT WE NEED OUR HEADS IN THE "NOW" -- EH?!
SKYWISE! TIMMAIN BROUGHT YOU...?
DREAMTIME Pt. 3
YEP! PICKED ME RIGHT UP FROM THE MOSS BED WHERE I WAS SNOOZING!
SHE "SENT" SOMETHING I DIDN'T QUITE CATCH. WHAT'S THIS ABOUT DREAMS?

ALL WHO SLEPT, WAITING TO REUNITE WITH YOU, ME AND THE TWINS -- THEY ARE BEGINNING TO REMEMBER, SKYWISE.
AH! NOW THAT COULD MAKE FOR AN INTERESTING LISTEN --
GRUMPH!
--O-O-O-RRR... THEN AGAIN... MAYBE NOT!
WHAT...? WANT ME TO COME WITH YOU, HIGH ONE?
SIGH ALL RIGHT... LET PIKE TAKE THOSE WHO WISH IT DOWN THE DARK DREAM PATH.
JUST DON'T COME BARKING TO ME IF SOMETHING BITES YOU ON THE WAY!
WHAT IN TIMMORN'S NAME DID YOU DREAM, OLDER BROTHER?
WHEW UPSETTING HIM IS THE LAST THING I WANT!
MY BELOVED'S TEMPER IS AS IT ALWAYS WAS... ONLY MORESO.
GIGGLE THAT "MORESO" EXTENDS TO OTHER THINGS, DOESN'T IT, SISTER?
AHEM! WELL, ZHANTEE, YOU HEARD HIM. GO ON! TELL US YOUR DREAM!

LESS EAGER THAN BEFORE, ZHANTEE WALKS THOUGHTFULLY... SILENTLY... FOLLOWED BY THOSE WITH WHOM HE FEELS THE MOST KINSHIP.
ARRIVING AT THE BARE SEA CLIFFS BEYOND THE FOREST'S EDGE, THE ELVES GAZE AT THE ROCK-BOUND SHORE OF THEIR NEW LAND.
BENEATH THE WAVES, WHERE THE WATER IS STILL, THE PALACE OF THE HIGH ONES LIES RESTING.
I MISS IT... MISS THE FEELING OF REALLY FLYING.
SOMEDAY MY SIRE, RAYEK, WILL RAISE IT FROM THE DEPTHS.
I KNOW HE WILL, VENKA! HE'LL MEET THE CHALLENGE.
BUT TILL THEN, WE MUST FLY IN OUR DREAMS.
ALL OF YOU... EVEN PIKE... YOU'RE THE ONLY ONES WHO CAN UNDERSTAND. I'M NOT REALLY A WOLFRIDER.
MY DREAM ISN'T DARK, LIKE REDLANCE'S OR TREESTUMP'S. NOTHING HINDERED ME. NOTHING I LOVED DIED.
CUTTER MIGHT TAKE OFFENSE--
--BECAUSE YOU SAW ONLY VISIONS OF LIGHT?! DON'T BE SILLY! GO ON!

"BUT I AM SILLY, HEALER... ALWAYS HAVE BEEN! PLACID AND SOFT AS THE ROLLING DUNES :HEH HEH...:
"IN MY SLEEP I SEE THEM OVER AND OVER AGAIN, THE DUNES... AS IF THE SUN IS MY HOME AND I LOOK DOWN ON THEM FROM HIGH IN THE BLAZING SKY.
"I SEE SORROW'S END TOO, OUR VILLAGE AND OUR FOLK. IT SEEMS I SWOOP DOWN TO THEM LIKE A DESERT HAWK ON THE WING.

"BUT, ONCE INSIDE THE VILLAGE, I SEE IT AS A CHILD WOULD... THE HUTS TOWERING ABOVE MY HEAD...
"... AND THE SURROUNDING MOUNTAINS, MUCH MUCH TALLER THAN THE HUTS.
"YET NOTHING LOOMS AND INVITES LIKE THE BRIDGE OF DESTINY!
"MOTHER, FATHER, THE RULING VOICES OF MY CHILDHOOD WARN, 'BE CAREFUL! DON'T GO UP THERE!'
"MUSN'T TAKE RISKS, LITTLE ONE, MUSN'T TRY TO TOUCH THE SKY!
"A GREAT 'NO' BARS MY WAY, RINGS IN MY DREAM-EARS. I FEEL HEAVY... ROOTED TO THE SPOT.

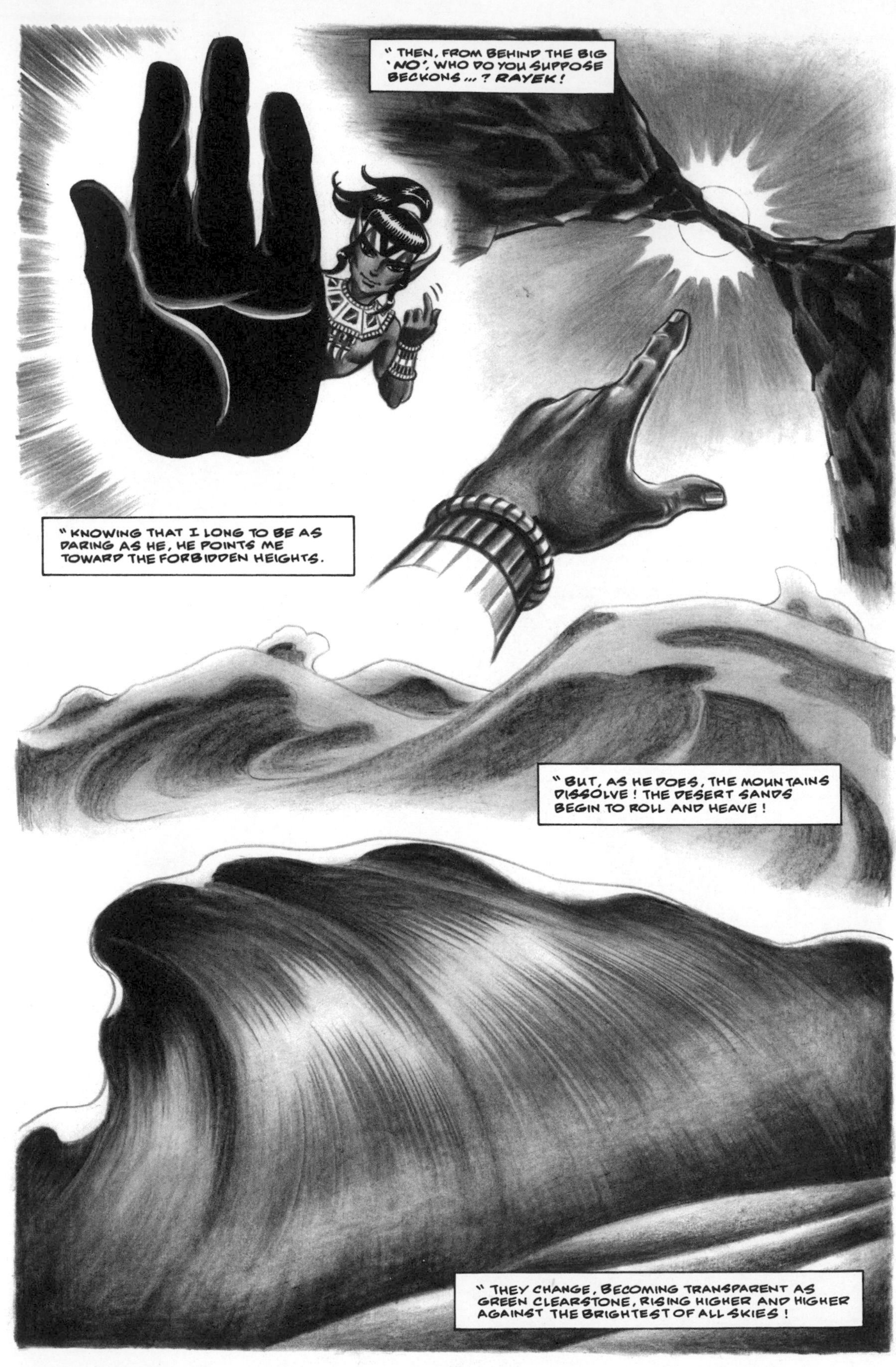
" THEN, FROM BEHIND THE BIG 'NO', WHO DO YOU SUPPOSE BECKONS ... ? RAYEK!
" KNOWING THAT I LONG TO BE AS DARING AS HE, HE POINTS ME TOWARD THE FORBIDDEN HEIGHTS.
" BUT, AS HE DOES, THE MOUNTAINS DISSOLVE! THE DESERT SANDS BEGIN TO ROLL AND HEAVE!
" THEY CHANGE, BECOMING TRANSPARENT AS GREEN CLEARSTONE, RISING HIGHER AND HIGHER AGAINST THE BRIGHTEST OF ALL SKIES!

" WATER... THE DESERT HAS TURNED ENTIRELY TO WATER! A SINGLE, ARCHING WAVE GATHERS FORCE AS IT RUSHES, HUGE BEYOND BELIEF, TOWARD SORROW'S END...
"... TOWARD ME! I DON'T EVEN TRY TO RUN. IT'S NO USE. THERE'S NO ESCAPE FOR THE VILLAGE OR ANYONE IN IT.
" I KNOW, BECAUSE I'VE SEEN THIS WAVE BEFORE... STOOD AND LET IT WASH OVER ME BEFORE... AS IT DOES NOW.

"AND JUST LIKE ALL THE OTHER TIMES, I'M NOT AFRAID."
BUT NONE OF US SUN FOLK EVER SAW THE VASTDEEP WATER, UNTIL NOW.
JUST DAYS AGO YOU SAVED ME... SHIELDED ME FROM SUCH A WAVE. PERHAPS THAT COLORS HOW YOU RECALL --?
--NO! THE REAL SEA FEELS...REAL! PAINFULLY SO!
BUT NEVER, IN MY SLEEP, ARE THERE THE DEADLY ROCKS OR NUMBING COLD.
THE DREAM-WAVE TUMBLES ME, BUT I CAN STILL BREATHE. IT'S NOT UNPLEASANT AT ALL.
HMMM... MUST BE A SYMBOL, THEN?
SOMEDAY I'LL KNOW WHAT IT MEANS.
IS THERE MORE?
MORE, SHENSHEN? :CHUCKLE: WELL, YES... IF YOUR SISTER WILL PARDON ME!
PART OF MY DREAM, AT LEAST, HAS COME TRUE SINCE OUR AWAKENING. NO MATTER HOW DEEP I PLUNGE, MY SHIELD PROTECTS ME.
BREATHING UNDER WATER IS LIKE FLYING, ONLY BETTER. HOW COULD EVEN WINNOWILL STAY SO BAD, WHEN IT FEELS SO WONDERFUL?

"AFTER THE DREAM-WAVE HITS, THE SUN VILLAGE IS FORGOTTEN. I KNOW THE OTHERS ARE LIKE ME NOW -- WEIGHTLESS, TIRELESS, LACKING NOTHING, FULL OF JOY.
"BUT THEN, LOOKING UP THROUGH THE BOTTOMLESS GREEN, I SEE A SHINING BALL -- THE DAYSTAR -- THE SUN!
"AND I REALIZE I STILL WANT SOMETHING... SOMETHING I KNOW IS THERE, ABOVE.
"SO I SWIM TOWARD IT...
"... AND FIND WHAT I SEEK...

"YOU, LEETAH. YOU ARE THE SUN!

"WITH ONE WARM, GENTLE HAND, YOU DRAW ME OUT OF THE WATER ... AND WITH THE OTHER YOU POINT THE WAY TO THE PALACE.
"YOU CHALLENGE ME TO KEEP GOING, EVEN THOUGH I WANT VERY MUCH TO STAY.
"FOR A MOMENT -- WE COME SO CLOSE --

"--WE PASS RIGHT THROUGH EACH OTHER! FOR THIS FEELING, THERE ARE NO WORDS. I -- I WON'T EVEN TRY.
"I CROSS THE SHINING PALACE'S THRESHOLD--
"--ONLY TO FIND DOORS... WITHIN DOORS... WITHIN DOORS!

IT SEEMS EACH ONE OPENS ON SUCH A BIG ADVENTURE, I DON'T EVER WANT TO TURN BACK!

YOU CAN ALL LAUGH NOW. IT IS A BIG-HEADED VISION FOR AN ELF LIKE ME.
I'M STILL NOT SURE WHY TIMMAIN CHOSE ME TO BE PART OF CUTTER'S BAND.

SURELY SHE SENSED THE POWER THAT SLEPT WITHIN YOU... THE POWER TO SHIELD OTHERS FROM HARM.
SHE KNEW, DESPITE YOUR SHYNESS, YOU'D BE ABLE TO KEEP UP WITH THE WOLFRIDERS...

"... AND THAT, COME WHAT MAY, YOU'D ALWAYS PUT THEIR NEEDS BEFORE YOUR OWN."

OH... I'M NOT SO NOBLE! IT'S JUST... THE WOLF-RIDERS MAKE THINGS HAPPEN... THINGS THAT MAKE ME STRETCH.
THOUGH OUR CHIEF'S GROWLS STILL UNNERVE ME, I GUESS I LIKE FACING ALL THE TESTS.

AND WHAT MORE THAN THAT DOES IT TAKE TO BE A TRUE WOLFRIDER?

YOU SAVED THE SUN THAT LIGHTS UP BOTH OUR LIVES.

SO WHAT'S THE IDEA OF EVEN QUESTIONING TIMMAIN'S CHOICE?
SNIFF

WHEN THIS GAME IS DONE, AND ALL THOSE PRECIOUS DREAM-STORIES ARE STRUNG TO-GETHER --
--WE NEED A SAFER PLACE THAN MY NUTSHELL OF A HEAD TO KEEP THEM!

PERHAPS THE SCROLL OF COLORS RECORDS WHAT WE DREAM, AS WELL AS WHAT WE DO.
MY FATHER MIGHT KNOW. IT'S TIME I RETURN TO HIM.
ZHANTEE, BEFORE YOU GO BACK--PLEASE TAKE ME TO RAYEK!

ANOTHER DAWN APPROACHES ON THE WORLD OF TWO MOONS ...
YET THE GENTLE GLOW THAT SUFFUSES THE COASTAL WATERS COMES NOT FROM THE SKY ABOVE, BUT FROM THE AURA SURROUNDING THE SUNKEN PALACE OF THE HIGH ONES.
AS A MAGICALLY SHIELDED ZHANTEE BEARS VENKA TO THE CRYSTALLINE STRUCTURE'S PORTAL ...
HEARING YOUR DREAM HELPED ME RECALL BITS OF MY OWN, LOVEMATE. FOR ME, THAT IS UNUSUAL.
I'M GLAD PIKE STARTED HIS DREAM-SHARING GAME.
ELSE I'D NEVER HAVE HAD THE NERVE TO TELL LEETAH HOW I --
DREAMTIME PATH

HEH HEH HEH I WOULDN'T WORRY. EVEN THE WOLVES KNOW HOW MUCH YOU MISSED HER.
AH! THERE'S FAITHFUL EKUAR... WAVING FROM THE DOOR.
MY LONELY SIRE IS FORTUNATE TO HAVE HIS COMPANY, JUST NOW.
ZHANTEE DIVES FOR THE SHIMMERING DOORWAY AND --

--PIERCES THE MEMBRANE WHICH HOLDS BACK THE MIGHTY, SALT FLOOD.
WELCOME CHILDREN, WELCOME! MIND THAT SLIPPERY FLOOR, NOW!
SIGH EACH ENTRY INTO THE PALACE IS AS WONDROUS AS THE FIRST!

WITHIN, MUSICAL CHATTER ECHOES...
ARE THE WOLFRIDERS WELL, DEAR VENKA? GROWING ACCUS-TOMED TO THE WORLD'S MANY CHANGES?
YES. SLOWLY. RED-LANCE IS RE-SHAPING OUR LONG OVERGROWN HOLT FROM THE BARE SOIL UP.

YOUNG ZHANTEE! WILL YOU NOT STAY AND VISIT?
SURELY... WHEN I RETURN WITH MORE SUPPLIES!
THANK YOU, LOVEMATE.

EKUAR... HOW IS...?
CLOSER TO DESPAIR THAN I'VE EVER SEEN HIM.

THE POWER TO MAKE THE PALACE FLY MEANT EVERYTHING TO POOR BROWNSKIN -- AND NOT JUST FOR SHOW.
HE TRULY INTENDED TO HELP THIS WORLD'S ELVES REGAIN THE GLORY OF THE HIGH ONES.
YET EVEN WHEN TIMMAIN, THE LIVING HIGH ONE, WOULD NOT SUPPORT HIS PLAN, HE REFUSED TO HEAR... TO SEE.
ONLY THE THOUGHT OF LOSING YOU GAVE HIM PAUSE AT LAST.

MOMENTS LATER...
RAYEK...?
DRIFTING... FLOATING... BUT NO VOLUNTARY MOVEMENT... NO TRACE OF EXPRESSION.
:AHEM: FATHER...?
YOU CANNOT KNOW WHAT A SHAME THIS IS, VENKA. WINNOWILL HAS BEEN MANY THINGS...
...BUT, ABOVE ALL, SHE WAS A CREATURE OF FIERCE AND FORCEFUL LIFE.
WHEN WILL SHE COME BACK TO ME?
I'VE A QUESTION FOR YOU.
DOES THE SCROLL OF COLORS RECORD DREAMS AS WELL AS DEEDS?

SIGH THAT I CANNOT TELL YOU.
YOU SEE... I'VE LOST THE POWER TO TURN THE SCROLL.
WHY DO YOU ASK?

WHILE WE SLEPT IN COCOONS OF PRESERVER WEBBING, OUR MINDS WERE NOT ALWAYS STILL.
PIKE IS COLLECTING OUR DREAMS. HE THINKS A COMMON THREAD BINDS THEM.
I THOUGHT, PERHAPS, BY READING THE SCROLL, WE MIGHT QUICKLY DISCOVER THAT THREAD AND THE WISDOM WOVEN THROUGH IT.
I DON'T UNDERSTAND...

HOW DID HE DO IT? HOW DID CUTTER CONVINCE ALL OF YOU TO SLEEP A GREAT PORTION OF YOUR LIVES AWAY... FOR HIS SAKE?
HE DID NOT. WE OFFERED.
WE LOVE HIM, YOU SEE.

THERE IS NO DIFFERENCE BETWEEN THE "NOW OF WOLF THOUGHT" AND IMMORTALITY.
IN EITHER STATE THE SENSE OF PASSING TIME IS ABSENT...
...EXCEPT FOR CUTTER.

HE ALONE FELT EACH DAY'S LOSS AS HE WAITED TO FIND HIS FAMILY AGAIN. FINALLY, HE COULD NO LONGER BEAR IT.
ALL HE EVER ASKED IS THAT WE FOLLOW HIM FREELY.
"WE DID. IT WAS THE LEAST WE COULD DO.
"THERE WAS NOTHING TO DREAD. THE TROLLS, PRESERVERS AND TIMMAIN WATCHED OVER US AND THE WOLF PACK AS WE SLEPT.
"SOMETIMES, WHEN OUR SOULS WERE NOT ADRIFT IN THE WORLD OF DREAMS, WE EVEN SENT TO EACH OTHER."
SO YOU SEE, IF SACRIFICE THERE WAS, IT WAS NOT SO TERRIBLE.
WHAT DID YOU DREAM?

HMMM... IT'S NOT SO EASY TO SORT VAGUE MEMORIES FROM SLEEP-VISIONS.
BUT I DO RECALL MY OLDEST NIGHTMARE... BRIEF... EVER REPEATING.
"FIRST I HEAR SOUNDS, LIKE BRITTLE THUNDER, CRASHING AND SMASHING OUTSIDE.
"THEN, WITH AN INFANT'S EYES I SEE A TERRIBLE THREAT FROM ABOVE.
"MY TINY HAMMOCK ROCKS WILDLY. BITS OF WOOD AND CLAY AND JAGGED STONE RAIN DOWN ON ME. STRIKE ME...
"...AND, THOUGH I SCREAM FOR MY VERY LIFE, NO ONE COMES TO MY AID!
"THAT'S ALL. IT SEEMS VERY REAL. BUT..."

I-- I THOUGHT YOU WERE DEAD! YOUR CURSED MOTHER, KAHVI, TOLD ME SO!
SO IT WAS YOU WHO ATTACKED THE LODGE... WITH ME IN IT!
BY THE DAYSTAR! IS THERE NO END TO MY ERRORS?!
VENKA...
IT'S ALL RIGHT. I DON'T THINK I'LL EVER HAVE THAT BAD DREAM AGAIN.
YOUR HATRED OF KAHVI... YOUR BANISHMENT OF THE GO-BACKS... ODD... SO ODD!
THESE THINGS ARE FRESH IN YOUR MIND. BUT I CAN ONLY DIMLY RECALL MY MOTHER'S FACE...
...IN MY OWN REFLECTION.
"IN TRUTH, SHE IS BUT HALF OF ME... THAT BOLD WARRIOR OF THE FROZEN MOUNTAINS. NOT FROM HER BREAST COMES WARMTH AND AFFECTION, FOR IT IS EN-CASED IN BITTER, COLD ARMOR.
"THE WARMTH I FIND IN MY OTHER HALF, THE HALF BORN OF THE DESERT. FIRES OF WISDOM AND INNER POWER BURN STEADILY, CONTAINED AND USEFUL."

"IN MY DREAM, THE MOTHER OF MEMORY REACHES OUT TO ME AND I REACH BACK.
"GENTLY, BUT FIRMLY, SHE PUSHES ASIDE THE HOWLING BERSERKER WHO WOULD FREEZE MY HEART AND USE ME AS HER TOOL OF VENGEANCE.
"WE TOUCH. I AM GOWNED LIKE HER ... CALM LIKE HER. WISDOM POURS INTO MY SOUL, ENDLESSLY, LIKE THE RAYS OF THE SUN.
"WE STAND ATOP A PLACE I KNOW TO BE THE BRIDGE OF DESTINY. IT IS MADE ALL OF FLAMES THAT LAP AT MY ANKLES ... BUT DO NOT BURN.

"THEN I HEAR MY MOTHER'S VOICE CALLING MY NAME. A FROSTY WIND CHILLS MY SPINE.
"HOW HEROIC SHE IS... HOW DETERMINED! NOW I AM DRAWN TO HER. SHE HAS LEARNED HOW TO GET WHAT SHE WANTS FROM ME.
"I TURN TO MEET KAHVI'S STARE. WHERE HER FEET TOUCH THE FIERY BRIDGE, ICE FORMS, FLOWING DOWN TO SNOW-CAPPED PEAKS.
"BEHIND HER, MISTY FIGURES -- THEY MUST BE GO-BACKS -- SEEM EAGER, ANTICIPATING HER NEXT MOVE.
"MOTHER HANDS ME HER SWORD AND SHIELD...

"... AND I, DELICATELY CLAD AS ANY MILD SUN VILLAGER, RISE ALOFT WITH THEM FROM THE BRIDGE!
"THE SHIELD, MINE TO CARRY WHEREVER I GO, IS WEIGHTLESS, ABLAZE WITH LIGHT, ITS PROTECTION UNDENIABLE.
"THE SWORD, NO MORE BURDENSOME THAN THE SHIELD, IS A TRANSPARENT SHARD OF ICE, CLEAR AND COOL AS REASON ITSELF.
"THUS ARMED, I RISE ABOVE THE CHEERING GO-BACKS -- WHO REVEAL WOLFRIDERS, TOO, AMONG THEIR RANKS."

OF COURSE YOU RISE ABOVE THEM! ANY FOOL CAN SEE YOU'RE--
--DON'T, FATHER.

YOU KNOW WHERE SUCH THINKING LEADS.
...YES. I CHOSE THE OBVIOUS. YOUR DREAM PROBABLY HAS FAR SUBTLER MEANING.

BUT I KNOW SO LITTLE OF YOU, VENKA. I--
--GO ON, BROWNSKIN! GO ON!

I ONLY HOPE THAT MEETING ME... HAS PLACED NO CONFLICT IN YOUR HEART.
MEETING YOU HAS RESOLVED IT.

SHORTLY, IN THORNY MOUNTAIN HOLT...
THAT VENKA IS A POWERFUL SENDER... ALL THE WAY FROM UNDER THE SEA!
INTERESTING DREAM TOO!
WE'VE RAISED HER AS ONE OF US, BUT SHE'S NEVER BEEN QUITE LIKE US.

AND YET SHE'S MORE A WOLFRIDER THAN SHE THINKS.
WHAT, BELOVED?
NOTHING. YOU KNOW.

AND ONLY YOU, FOR I'VE TOLD NO ONE ELSE HOW KAHVI INTERRUPTED MY LONG SLUMBER...
...NOT YET.

THE SUN IS UP, TRIBEMATES, OR HADN'T YOU NOTICED?
TIME TO LAY ASIDE PIKE'S IDLE GAME AND GET SOME SIMPLE, PRACTICAL REST.
HOPEFULLY WITHOUT ANY DREAMS FOR ONCE!

REDLANCE... NIGHTFALL...
WILL YOU "TREE" WITH US TODAY?
OH...! WE WOULDN'T THINK OF INTRUDING, LEETAH!
YOU AND CUTTER HAVE BEEN REUNITED SUCH A SHORT WHILE...
HEY! YOU'RE MY FAMILY TOO.
AND MINE. PLEASE COME WITH US.
HO HUM! I GUESS THE FURS ARE CALLING...
AND...
LOOK AT HIM! CUTTER FLIES FROM BRANCH TO BRANCH AS MERRILY AS A PRESERVER!
HA HA HAH! ARE YOU THAT SLEEPY? YOU CLIMB LIKE BABY TREEWEES!
CREAK!
SKSSHH!

WHISSHH!
I NEVER DARED HOPE TO SEE HIM SO HAPPY AGAIN!

HOW CAN I REVEAL A SECRET THAT MIGHT TROUBLE HIM ANEW?
THUMPF!

BUT, AS THE DROWSY DAY PASSES, NOTHING CAN LONG STAY HIDDEN AMONG LOVING FRIENDS...
SO THE GO-BACKS CARRY A DROP OF WOLF BLOOD FROM TWO-SPEAR'S TIME! A DROP SO THIN, NONE OF US COULD SCENT IT!
HOW CAN I THANK YOU, NIGHTFALL? YOU SHIELDED CUTTER FROM KAHVI'S GREED EVEN AS I WOULD.
DON'T THINK TWICE OF IT. I DIDN'T.
LIFEMATE... LOVEMATES... TRIBEMATES... YOU'RE ALL ONE TO ME. THERE'S NOTHING I WOULDN'T DO FOR YOU...

...SO LONG AS I'M ABLE!

PEACEFUL EVENING - DAYBREAK TO THE NOCTURNAL WOLFRIDERS - DESCENDS ON THORNY MOUNTAIN HOLT...
NIGHTFALL AND REDLANCE'S GENTLE DAUGHTER, ARISEN WELL BEFORE HER PARENTS, LOOKS AFTER THE TRIBE'S YOUNGEST MEMBERS.
SEE, TYLEET? THE MOONHATCHERS! THEY'RE FINALLY HERE!
WAAK WAAAK WAK WAK
SO TINY! SO BRAVE! LISTEN TO THEIR MOTHER CALL THEM!
OH-OH-OH! LOOK! THE FIRST ONE'S GETTING READY TO JUMP!
DREAMTIME
PT 5
SHHH, EMBER! DON'T FRIGHTEN THEM!
AH... A RARE SIGHT!

PEEP PEEP PEEP PEEP PEEP
"COURAGE IS BORN IN THOSE LITTLE ONES, TO MAKE THAT FIRST, TERRIBLE LEAP UNAIDED!"
AYOOOAH!!
GOOD JUMP!
KWOK KWOK KWOK
PLUNK!

FOUR... FIVE...SIX... Whew! THEY ALL MADE IT!
RLOPP!
KERPLUNK!
PEEP PEEP PEEP
SPLOOSH!
YES, SUNTOP! A HARD WAY TO BEGIN LIFE, ISN'T IT?
BUT THEIR MOTHER'S PROUD! THEY'VE PROVED THEY'RE STRONG!

A MOTHER IS ALWAYS PROUD OF HER YOUNG.
BE THEY HELPLESS AT BIRTH OR NO, SHE'LL GUARD THEM WITH HER LIFE--

--UNTIL THEY'RE NO LONGER CHILDREN. UNTIL THEY'RE BIG ENOUGH TO BE CALLED **FRIENDS**!
NEVER TOO BIG TO CUDDLE UNDER MOTHER'S WING NOW AND THEN!

TIME TO GO!
OOOWWWOOOOOOOOOOOO!

SWIFTLY, NIGHTFALL'S CHOSEN HUNTING PARTNERS RESPOND TO HER CALL.

Pant Pant Pant

WHUFF!

PHEW!! THAT'S WORSE THAN USUAL!

WHAT IN TIMMORN'S NAME HAVE YOU BEEN **ROLLING** IN?!

WHO, NIGHTFALL?

YOUR WOLF-FRIEND?

OR **ME**?

Sniff Sniff

I'M NOT SO SURE, **PIKE**!

OH, WELL... WE'LL ALL SMELL ALIKE SOON ENOUGH!

Heh Heh Heh...

YOU'VE GOT **THAT** RIGHT!

LET'S GO!

YOU KNOW...
...YOU NEVER GOT AROUND TO TELLING ME YOUR DREAM.
SO, YOU'VE FINALLY DECIDED IT'S MY TURN, EH?
SORRY...
...NO!
YOU GAVE ME TIME TO PONDER.
NOW THAT I'VE HEARD SOME OF THE OTHERS' DREAMS, I SEE WHERE MINE FITS IN.
"IN MY SLEEP I OFTEN RELIVED THOSE HAPPY DAYS WHEN TYLEET AND VENKA WERE LITTLE CUBS.
"MY DREAM-HOLT SEEMS MORE THAN BEAUTIFUL, THE TREES TALLER, THE FLOWERS BRIGHTER...
"...THOUGH NOT SO BRIGHT AS MY DEAR ONES' SMILES.
"THEN... REDLANCE COMES TO ME, BEARING A SINGLE, SAD, WITHERED FLOWER IN HIS HANDS.
"HE BEGINS TO WORK HIS TREE-SHAPING MAGIC...

"...AND SOON THE FLOWER BLOOMS AGAIN, GROWING AND GROWING...
"...UNTIL, NURTURED BY ALL OUR LOVE, IT TAKES FORM...
"...AS CUTTER!
"HIS RENEWED POWER SPEARS THROUGH THE HOLT LIKE PAINLESS SKYFIRE, GIVING VIGOR TO ALL LIVING THINGS--UNITING US ALL IN THE WAY.
"AS OUR CHIEF THRIVES, SO THRIVES THE TRIBE...

"...AND WE KNOW THE JOY OF AIDING HIM, AS FRIENDS OF HIS BODY AND SPIRIT!
"BUT THEN...
"...A DARK SHADOW SLINKS FROM THE FOREST. IT'S COME TO DIM THE LIGHT OF OUR PEACE!
"I **KNOW** THIS SHADOW. IT HUNGERS FOR WHAT WE HAVE.
"AND IT HAS NO EYES TO SEE THE DREADFUL HARM IT WILL WREAK AS IT SATISFIES ITS NEED.
"THE COLD, GREEDY SHADE FEEDS ON CUTTER'S **STRENGTH**, DRAWING HIM IN...
"...AWAY FROM US!

"I SEE THE FOREST FADING, THE WAY FADING...
"...CUBS, CHIEF AND LIFEMATE ALL CONSUMED BY THAT RAVENOUS SHADOW!
"NO! NOT WHILE MY STEADY ARM CAN STILL FIRE ONE, CLEAN SHOT!
"MY ARROW TEARS THE DARK THING AT ITS CORE!
"BUT THERE IS NO DEATH SCREAM. WHAT I HEAR...
"...IS LAUGHTER.
"THE SHREDS OF SHADOW WRITHE AND REFORM. AND I RECOGNIZE THESE SHAPES TOO.
HA HA HA HA HA HA
"THESE ARE THE USERS AMONG OUR OWN KIND... THE LOVELESS ONES..."

"...WITHOUT PITY...
"...WITHOUT LOYALTY...
"...WITHOUT REGARD FOR THE HOPES AND WISHES OF ANY BUT THEMSELVES.
"WITH THESE SHADOW MEMBERS OF OUR RACE BEGINS THE HOLT'S DOWNFALL!
"NO OTHERS ARE TO BLAME! THE FAULT IS OURS!
HA HA
HA HA
HA HA
HA HA
"YET I'LL FIGHT THEM TO THE LAST, PIERCE THEIR DARKNESS THREE TIMES OVER TO SAVE WHAT I LOVE MOST!

"THREE ARROWS FLY!
"AND ALL THREE FIND THEIR MARK!
"WOUNDED, THE DARK ONES RETREAT WITH WHAT'S LEFT OF MY FAMILY AND VENKA!
"AND BARRING MY PATH, A CROWD OF HUMANS APPEARS... FEEDING LIKE CARRION BIRDS ON THE LAST, LIFE-DRAINED TWIGS OF MY HOME!
"I WON'T GIVE UP!
"I GIVE CHASE, RIGHT THROUGH THAT WALL OF SCAVENGING HUMANS...
"...INTO THE DEEPEST, COLDEST EMPTINESS I'VE EVER KNOWN!

"REDLANCE...!
"CUTTER...!
'CUBS!
"NOW I'M IN THE GO-BACKS' LODGE, FACING THE LOVELESS ONES WHO'VE RESTORED THEMSELVES BY FEEDING ON THEIR CAPTIVES' SPIRITS!
"THIS IS THE PLACE WHERE REDLANCE FOUGHT ALONE, DURING THE PALACE WAR, BECAUSE I COULDN'T BE THERE TO HELP HIM!
"WELL, I'M HERE NOW...!

"AND FOR WHAT THEY'VE DONE TO MY LIFEMATE, WHO *IS* THE HOLT...
"...TO CUTTER, WHO *IS* THE WAY...
"...AND TO THE PRECIOUS CUBS WHO ARE OUR TRIBE'S ONE *PROMISE* OF *SURVIVAL*...
"...I WILL TAKE TERRIBLE *REVENGE*!
"*WINNOWILL*...!
"*RAYEK*...!
"*TWO EDGE*...!
"AND *YOU*, HUNGRY, LURKING SHADOW...!

"I'LL DESTROY YOU ALL!

"MY QUIVER IS BOTTOMLESS... MY ARROWS A **PIERCING HAIL!**

HA HA

HA HA

"BUT THE INFURIATING LAUGHTER GOES ON!

HA HA

HA HA HA

"THE SHADOWS ONLY GROW **LARGER** AS THEIR CAPTIVES SHRIVEL, ALMOST TO NOTHING!

"HOW CAN I SAVE THEIR LIVES?! **HOW?!!**

"THEN... THE **ANSWER** COMES, CLEAR AS MORNING DEWDROPS. WHY DIDN'T I THINK OF IT BEFORE?!

"JUST AS **TRIUMPH** SEEMS WITHIN MY GRASP...

"...EVERYTHING **VANISHES**! AND I **FORGET** WHAT IT WAS I MIGHT HAVE DONE TO SAVE MY DEAR ONES!

"THAT WAS THE MOMENT **KAHVI**, MISTAKING ME FOR CUTTER, SLICED OPEN MY COCOON--

--AND WOKE ME. I THINK **SHE** HERSELF CAUSED MY DREAM.

SOMEHOW... I MUST HAVE SENSED HER COMING.

Wheeeew!

SCARY! NONE OF US, NOT EVEN STRONGBOW, HAS EVER OUTMATCHED YOUR WILL TO PROTECT.

DO YOU SEE, NOW, HOW MY DREAM FITS IN... AT LEAST WITH **REDLANCE'S** AND **TREESTUMP'S**?
Hmmm... I GUESS WE PURE-BLOODED WOLFRIDERS CAN'T HELP BUT SHARE THE SAME WORRIES.
STILL, THERE'S MORE TO IT THAN THAT, OR THERE'S **NO** FIGURING **MY** DREAM IN!

WAIT'LL YOU HEAR-- Eh?!
Sniff Sniff

NIGHTFALL... JUST BEYOND THOSE BUSHES! **A TUSK HOG!**
Whuff

HEY! WHERE ARE YOU GOING?
IT'S... JUST NOT IN ME TO KILL TONIGHT, PIKE. SORRY.
DON'T TAKE ON THAT TUSK HOG ALONE. SEND FOR THE OTHERS.
Hmph!

THERE IS A SACRED PACT BETWEEN HUNTER AND PREY. BOTH MUST BE UP FOR THE HUNT, OR IT'S NO GOOD.
BUT THERE ARE THOSE, LIKE THE MOON HATCHERS, WHO CAN USE AND THROW RARE THINGS AWAY WITHOUT CARING.

MOTHER! BACK SO SOON?
giggle! TICKLES, HUH, EMBER?
KWOK KWOK KWOK

THERE'S A TIME TO KILL... AND A TIME TO SIT AND WATCH--

--THE BEAUTY WE SOMETIMES FORGET TO SEE...

JUST PAST A TANGLE OF BUSHES, ONE OF THORNY MOUNTAIN HOLT'S MOST VICIOUS DENIZENS ROOTS FOR GRUBS...
Humph! NIGHTFALL MUST THINK FACE FUR MEANS NOTHING MORE THAN A WARM CHIN!
"DON'T TAKE ON THAT TUSK-HOG ALONE, PIKE."
RUNK RUNK RUNK
I'LL SHOW 'ER!
I'LL CATCH IT WITH MY BARE HANDS!
CHONK!
whi-i-i-ine...?
COME ON, TREMBLY BONES, DON'T BE SUCH A RABBIT!

RUNK RUNK
FOOF
RUNK RUNK RUNK
GOTCHA!
REEEEEEEEEEEE!!
WOA!
RRRURRRH!
WHOA!
RREEEUUURR!
I SAID WHOA!
SNORT
WOOPFF!!
SNORT SNORT!

OOF!
UFF!
OOF!
HRRRRUUUUURRR!

Whine Whine
DON'T WORRY...!
I GOT 'IM
Unh --

--RIGHT WHERE
oopf
I WANT 'IM
unh!
SNORT SNORT SNORT

GASP!!!

YAAAH!

SSSKSSSHH!!

EEYOWFF!
BAP!
RRRRRRRH!

UUNH!!
AUGH!!
KLUDD!!

???
YOU ROCK-BRAIN! THAT ROOT COULD'VE BUSTED YOUR TAIL!
WHERE'S YOUR SPEAR?! AND WHY WERE YOU HUNTING ALONE?

I HAD 'IM, CUTTER, 'TIL YOU CAME ALONG!
SURE YOU DID!
TUSK-HOGS AREN'T SO TOUGH TO CATCH. YOU JUST GOTTA THINK LIKE 'EM!

FOR YOU THAT SHOULD BE EASY!
COME ON! I'LL SHOW YOU HOW TO SNAG ONE WITHOUT A WEAPON!
Sniff snuffle

sniff sniff
HMMM... HE WENT THAT WAY. BUT LET ME MAKE THE CATCH.
I WANT TO PROVE TO NIGHTFALL IT CAN BE DONE SINGLE-HANDED!

THIS I MUST SEE!
HER DREAM WAS A REAL FOOT-FLAILER, BY THE WAY...
...FULL OF THREATS AND DANGER TO FAMILY AND HOLT.

SOUNDS BAD AS BEING AWAKE!
UH-UH. THERE WAS HOPE. HER DREAM WAS TRYING TO SHOW HER HOW TO WIN...
...BUT KAHVI WOKE HER BEFORE IT COULD.

DREAMS NEVER MEAN ANYTHING... NEVER SOLVE ANYTHING.

YOU DON'T BELIEVE THAT. AND I SURE DON'T--
--NOT AFTER THE ONE I HAD!

"JUST PICTURE IT...! THE TROLLS HAVE BROUGHT A GREAT VAT OF DREAMBERRIES INTO THE HOLT! EVERYBODY'S SILLY ON FRESH-TROMPED WINE!
"I'M DANCING IN THE VAT WITH SOME HALF-CLOTHED TROLL LOVELIES... SQUISHING THE BERRIES WITH MY FEET... FEELING THE JUICE RUNNING BETWEEN MY TOES!
"WE'RE ALL LAUGHING AND SINGING! IT'S A GUZZLE-NUZZLE PARTY!
"}snerk{ I'VE SWALLOWED SO MANY CRUSHED BERRIES--
"--EVEN THE TROLL MAIDENS LOOK BEAUTIFUL TO ME!
"THAT IS, 'TIL ALL THE HUGGING AND LIP-SMUSHING STARTS!
"YOUCH! I'M BEING SQUOOSHED LIKE A DREAMBERRY!"

snort WHAT A PREDICAMENT!
SHH!
SMELL 'IM? TUSK-HOG'S GONE TO GROUND --RIGHT THERE!

ALL WE HAVE TO DO IS LURE 'IM OUT.
SO... STICK YOUR RUMP IN THE MOUTH OF HIS DEN. SEE WHAT HAPPENS.

VERY FUNNY...
...BUT NOT A BAD IDEA!

YOU'RE FOOLING, RIGHT?
STAND BACK! JUST WATCH THE EXPERT!
THAT NASTY OINKER WON'T BE ABLE TO RESIST THE "GAME"!
I'LL SENSE HIS CHARGE, JUMP UP, AND CATCH HIS NECK IN A LEG LOCK!

YOUR BACK END'S THAT SMART, HUH?
WHY AM I NOT SURPRISED?

QUITE A BIT LATER...
sigh GREAT PLAN, PIKE. HE'S SURE TAKING THE BAIT.
BE PATIENT.
SO... THE TROLL MAIDENS...?
WHAT ABOUT 'EM?
OH, MY DREAM.
YEAH...

"WELL, THEY'RE SMOTHERING ME, YOU KNOW? AND THE TRIBE'S NO HELP... BUNCH OF HOWLING HOOT OWLS!
"I HAVE TO ESCAPE. BUT HOW?
"SEEMS LIKE THE ONLY WAY IS TO GET... SMALLER!
"SO I DO! JUST THAT! SMALLER...
"...AND SMALLER...
"...'TIL, AT LAST, I WRIGGLE FREE OF THE TROLL MAIDENS' CLUTCHES...
"...AND SINK DOWN AMONG ALL THOSE LUSCIOUS BERRIES! YUMMM!
"HIDING THERE, I KNOW I'M SAFE.
"BUT NO! THEY COME DIGGING FOR ME!
"AT MY SIZE, IF THEIR BIG, FAT PAWS GRAB ME--"
RRRR....UUUURRR....
--THEY'LL POP MY HEAD LIKE A SEED POD!

"SO I'VE GOT TO GET SMALLER STILL. IN FACT... I GET ***SO*** SMALL--

"--I TURN ***INTO A DREAMBERRY!***"

chuckle

dum dee dee dum

BOINK!

"***NOW*** ESCAPE IS EASY. I JUST BOUNCE RIGHT OUT OF A LITTLE HOLE IN THE VAT...

"...AND ONTO THE FOREST FLOOR!

"BUT..."

DOINK!

BOINK!

AHH! C'MERE, RIPE 'N' JUICY!
"OH, NO!

"OH, NO!!"

NOOOOO!!

SNORT SNORT
RRRRUUNK!
WOO!! IT'S HIM!!
POP
HUH?!
BOMPH!
REEEEEEE!
OOOFF!!
...MOTHER...!
C'MON! TWIST 'IS NECK!
HELP ME BREAK IT!
SNURT! SNURT!
GRURRFF!
OH, RIGHT!

HE'S SPINNING-- EEYAAAH!
pant pant pant
UNNGH! GUH!

CUTTER! LET GO!
...AND... ...GET... ...TUSK-SPLIT?!!

THOOMP!
OH NO! FOR TIMMORN'S SAKE, LET GO!

CAN'T! -- STUCK IN HIS DEN-DOOR hnnnh!
HE'LL GOUGE MY FACE OFF!

ALL RIGHT... ALL RIGHT... STAY CALM!
THERE'S ALWAYS A WAY OUT!
DISTRACT 'IM, SO I CAN YANK YOU FREE!

pant gasp
DISTRACT 'IM... FINALLY --SOMETHING I CAN USE!
GEGGRRRRRRURRUURRRRGH!!

LISTEN, PIKE...

...WHEN I SAY "PULL..."

ZHLOOP!
GAAAK!
PULL!!

HUFF! THERE!!
EEYOW!!
CHOKE! KOFF!

RUUUUN!
splutter
HRRUUURGH!
OH, PUCKER-NUTS!

pant pant
ALWAYS A WAY OUT, HUH?
ALWAYS! puff pant THAT'S WHAT MY DREAM TAUGHT ME.

TAUGHT YOU? A POKING TROLL ATE YOU!

I ESCAPED.
HOW?

HOW DO YOU THINK?

sigh OH, DUNG!
THAT'S EXACTLY RIGHT, MY CHIEF...

POOT
DOINK
tee hee hee
"THAT'S EXACTLY RIGHT...!"

OOF!
GET OUT OF MY TREE! JUST... GET OUT OF MY TREE!!
REEEEEeeee- UNKH!!
Heh Heh Heh...
pant pant
Whurf!
Heh Heh Heh Heh...
LOSE SOMETHING, LIFEMATE?
YIPE!
SSSHOKK!
KRIM... SKOT... NICE KILL!
THANKS!
AND...
WELL, PIKE. YOU SAY ALL OUR DREAMS MEAN SOMETHING...
...AND SOMEDAY YOU'RE GOING TO FIGURE OUT HOW THEY ALL FIT TOGETHER.
I SAY YOU'VE PROVED JUST ONE THING...
YOU CAN ONLY DREAM ABOUT WHAT YOUR HEAD'S STUFFED FULL OF!

PIKE'S RECENT TUSK-HOG KILL IS DIVIDED AMONG THE TRIBE AND WOLF PACK. THE MEAT IS WARM AND RED.
BEFORE THE NIGHT IS DONE, **EVERY** PART OF THE KILL WILL HAVE BEEN EATEN OR SET ASIDE FOR OTHER USES.
DREAMTIME
UUMMM! LET'S CELEBRATE OUR AWAKENING WITH THE **SMELL** OF SMOKE AND THE **SIZZLE** OF FAT!
I LIKE MY MEAT CHARRED, **NOT** STILL BREATHING!

NO USE TREADING THAT OLD PATH AGAIN, KRIM.
NO FIRE!
WE'VE BARELY STARTED SCOUTING OUR TERRITORY.
THERE'S NO TELLING HOW STRONG THE "TALL ONES" HAVE GROWN WHILE WE SLEPT.

AND REDLANCE HASN'T BEGUN TO RESHAPE OUR THORN WALL.
NOTHING WE DO MUST GIVE OUR PRESENCE AWAY TO THE HUMANS!

YOU NEVER DID KNOW HOW TO SAY "POKE IT" AND THROW A REAL FEAST, CUTTER!
WOLFRIDERS HAVE NO GIFT FOR MERRY-MAKING --NOT LIKE US GO-BACKS!

HMPH!
HERE WE GO AGAIN!
HIDING OUR TAILS AND WATCHING FOR HUMANS UNDER EVERY ROCK!
AS LONG AS YOU'VE BRED YOUR SHARE OF YOUNG, WHAT'S SO THUMPING IMPORTANT ABOUT KEEPING ALIVE?

YOU AND I SEE IT THAT WAY, SKOT. CUTTER NEVER WILL. GET USED TO IT.
BESIDES, WE HAVEN'T BRED OUR SHARE YET! NO POINT IN SEEKING A WARRIOR'S DEATH 'TIL -- HEY!
THERE!
HALFWAY DOWN THE MOUNTAIN--

"--SMOKE!"
"A CAMPFIRE!"

sn-i-i-ifff AAAAHHH...!
ROAST DEER MEAT... slurp

chuckle WE'RE GONNA BE BAD, AREN'T WE?
IT'S WHAT WE DO BEST!
ROUND-EARS OR NO ROUND-EARS--

--THAT ROAST IS OURS!

SOON...
BU-U-U-RRUPP!
HI, PETAL-WING!
WHAT A FEED MY LIFEMATES MISSED! THERE'S NOTHING LEFT!

yawn THINK I'LL GO TEASE 'EM ABOUT IT.
I'D NEVER GO BELLY-EMPTY JUST TO KICK AGAINST THE RULES!

GUESS THEY'RE STILL SULKING IN OUR TREE-DEN ...
sniff sniff
HUH?! NO SCENTS... NO SOUNDS... NO SKOT AND KRIM!
NOW, WHERE IN...?

APPREHENSIVE, PIKE TRACKS HIS LIFEMATES PARTWAY DOWN THE MOUNTAIN, WHERE...
UH OH! SMOKE...FROM SOME HUMAN'S COOK-FIRE!
SKOT... KRIM...TELL ME YOU'RE NOT THAT WITLESS!

OF COURSE YOU ARE! I KNOW YOU!
YOU WANT IT, YOU GO GET IT--
--AND DUNGBALLS IN THE FACE OF ANY NO-SAYER!
WELL, I WON'T TELL ON YOU...

"I JUST HOPE I DON'T HAVE TO SAVE YOUR STUBBORN NECKS!"
<BE MORE FAITHFUL WITH YOUR TURNING, DUNYONK.>
<LOOK THERE! YOU'VE GONE AND BLACKED OUR SUPPER ON ONE SIDE!>
<Heh Heh Heh... AND WOULD YOU WED ME, WERE I TO MAKE A BETTER JOB OF IT?>
BWAAH HAH HAH!
<C'MON! GIVE US A KISS!>
smack smack
WHO NEEDS TO? THEY DON'T LOOK HALF AS TOUGH AS I REMEMBER.
CAN'T UNDERSTAND A WORD OF THEIR CHATTER.
snicker WE'LL MAKE 'EM MESS THEIR BREECHES.
POKE THAT! JUST MAKE 'EM RUN!

AAAYOOOOAHH!!
HUUUAAAAAAH!!!
Gasp
FLY, ROUND-EARS!!
FLY OR DIE!!
SKOT DIVES FOR THE NEAREST WOODSMAN, EXPECTING THE HUMAN TO FIGHT...

...NOT TO COLLAPSE IN ASTONISHMENT!
KRUMPF!
THE FLAMES !!!
CRACKLE!
AAAAGH!!
<POOR LAD!>
<HIS TUNIC'S ABLAZE!>
UNH!
AAAGH!
HUNH!
THEY'RE CLOSING IN FOR THE KILL!

NOOOOOO!!
AAAYOOOOOOOAAH!!!
SKOT! KRIM!
< THREKSH'T ABOVE! WHAT'S HAPPENING?! >
< SPIRITS! >
< FOREST SPIRITS! WE'VE ANGERED THEM! >
< THEY'RE AFTER US! RUN!! >
PAT
PAT
PAT
PAT
OH! OOW!
FIRE'S OUT! STRIP 'IM!
Uuuunhh...
gasp HIGH ONES...!
MOMENTS LATER...
C'MON, GNAWBONES, GIMME THAT HAUNCH!
RRR-RRR-RRRH
WE NEED THE FAT TO DRESS SKOT'S BURNS!

SOON...
KRIM!
GO ON AHEAD! TELL LEETAH TO BE READY!
RIGHT! DON'T BE LONG!

YOU'RE... YOU'RE NOT ANGRY...?
WHY?
THOSE BURNS ARE NOTHING TO THE ROASTING CUTTER'LL GIVE YOU!

I KNOW...
NNGH!

hsss

EASY...

BETWEEN YOU AND ME-- hss --IF I HAD TO CHOOSE A WAY TO GO--
--I'D PICK FIRE LAST!

"DON'T THINK OF THE PAIN, SKOT. I KNOW...! TELL ME A DREAM!"

DREAM?! YOU AND YOUR GAME!
"DOES A WOLF WHO RUNS IN HIS SLEEP REMEMBER WHAT IT WAS HE THOUGHT HE WAS CHASING?
"GO-BACKS DON'T REMEMBER SLEEP-PICTURES. JUST BEING ALIVE IS LIKE WALKING THROUGH A SNOW-DREAM ANYWAY.
"WHAT'S BEHIND VANISHES IN WHITE. WHAT'S AHEAD IS COVERED IN WHITE.
"ALL YOU CAN SEE IS YOUR FEET, MOVING ONE IN FRONT OF THE OTHER. THAT'S ALL THAT MATTERS.

"YOU KEEP GOING 'TIL IT'S TIME TO STOP. AND WHEN YOU DO--

"--YOU SEE WHAT'S BEFORE AND WHAT'S BEHIND WERE ALWAYS PRETTY MUCH THE SAME.

"ALL THAT ***EVER*** MATTERED WAS THE GOING. WHEN YOU CAN'T DO IT ANY MORE--

"--THE ***NEXT*** ONE TAKES YOUR PLACE.

"THAT'S MY ***ONLY*** DREAM, PIKE, WAKING OR SLEEPING--

"--TO MAKE A ***FAWN*** WHO'LL TAKE MY PLACE--

"--SO I CAN STOP.

"MY SPIRIT WILL GO BACK TO THE PALACE AND DWELL WITH THE OTHERS WHO'VE GONE BEFORE."

Heh Heh... WE'LL GIVE ***RAYEK*** SUCH A HARD TIME, HE'LL GIVE UP TRYING TO BE A HIGH ONE FOR G--***UUUH!***

SHH! IT'S ALL RIGHT! WE MADE IT!

AND...

⊰sigh⊱ HEALER, I ALWAYS SAID YOUR HANDS WERE AS SOOTHING AS WARM--

--MIL-KK!!

SMACK!

YOU **FOOL**! AFTER SLEEPING THE HIGH ONES KNOW **HOW MANY YEARS**--

--YOU'D **THROW** YOUR LIFE AWAY ON A COOKED LEG OF DEER!!

YOU WERE **SEEN** BY HUMANS! WORSE, YOU **ATTACKED** THEM!
IF THE OLD HATES **ENDED** WHILE WE SLEPT, **YOU'VE** STIRRED THEM UP AGAIN!
GIVE ME ONE GOOD REASON NOT TO DRIVE YOU BOTH OUT-- **FOREVER**!

PLEASE, CUTTER! WE **WOLFRIDERS** LEARNED TO CARE ABOUT WHAT'S **BEEN** AND WHAT'S **TO BE**.
BUT SKOT AND KRIM **NEVER** DID.

THINK OF THE DREAMS YOU'VE HEARD SO FAR-- SO MANY FEARS FROM YESTERDAY-- AND FEARS FOR TOMORROW.
SOME OF US FIGHT THEM...
SOME OF US FALL TO THEM...
SOME OF US FLEE FROM THEM...
AND SOME OF US FLY ABOVE THEM!
FEARS MAKE US WANT TO PROTECT WHAT WE HAVE ... SO WE CAN KEEP GOING.
BUT SKOT AND KRIM LIVE A PART OF THE WAY WE'VE LOST SIGHT OF.
THEY TRULY LIVE IN THE "NOW OF WOLF THOUGHT."
CUTTER... DON'T BLAME THEM FOR THAT.
grrr...
VERY WELL.

ALL THE SAME...
MOON-SHADE AND I WILL TAKE THESE TWO IN HAND!
THE WAY HAS OTHER WISDOM THEY NEED REMINDING OF!
OWTCH!

NICE SHOT, LEETAH!
.....

SHOW SOME RESPECT!
I WAS!
I LIKE IT WHEN OUR CHIEF AND HEALER BEAR THEIR FANGS!

THEN YOU'RE GOING TO LOVE DEALING WITH ME!

IN A SHALLOW STONE PIT FORMED BY EKUAR THE ROCK-SHAPER, TWO DEERSKINS CURE IN A REEKING SOLUTION OF TREE BARK, LEGLIFT WATER AND BRINE.
GRUDGINGLY, UNDER THE CRITICAL GAZE OF TRIBAL TANNER MOONSHADE, GO-BACK MAIDEN KRIM DOES PENANCE FOR LAST NIGHT'S DELIBERATE MISBEHAVIOR.
...THEN, AFTER TWO FULL CHANGES OF MOTHER MOON, WE'LL TAKE THE HIDES OUT, POUND AND STRETCH THEM.
PHEW! I'D RATHER BE SNIFFING MOONS-OLD FISH GUTS!
SCRAPE SCRAPE SCRAPE
THIS IS AS FAR FROM MY FAVORITE PASTIME AS YOU COULD GET ME!
DREAMTIME PART 8
THAT'S THE IDEA. KEEP SCRAPING!

SHOW BY YOUR DEEDS THAT YOU'RE TRULY SORRY FOR REVEALING YOURSELF TO THE HUMANS--
--AND CUTTER JUST MIGHT FORGIVE YOU.
WILL YOU...?
WE'LL SEE.

Heh Heh Heh...
...THAT FLOWERLIKE FACE NEVER FOOLED ME, MOONSHADE!
HARD AS BRIGHTMETAL, AREN'T YOU?
NOT SO HARD AS STRONGBOW!

"YOU CAN THANK THE HIGH ONES YOU'RE NOT IN SKOT'S BOOTS RIGHT NOW!"
THERE! YOU'VE SEEN IT MANY TIMES.
GRRRRR!
GROWRR!
THE CHIEF WOLF PUTS DOWN REBELLION WITHIN THE PACK.
OW! CUT IT OUT!

I TOLD YOU! NO TALKING! SEND!
BAP!
NOW, IF THE LOW-RANKING WOLF IS TOO STUBBORN TO SUBMIT--

GRURRR-RRR!
YIII YIII YIII
"--THE ONE'S HIGHER UP WILL LEAVE HIM BLOODY... OR WORSE!"
SNARRRGLE!

LEARN FROM THIS!
GO TO CUTTER. SHOW HIM THROAT.
wimper whine
lap lap lap

IF YOU DON'T, AT YOUR SLIGHTEST NEXT SLIP, HE'LL CAST YOU OUT!
AND NONE OF US WILL DEFEND YOU!

UNDER-STOOD...?
URGH! I HATE TRYING TO SEND! IT MAKES MY HEAD ACHE!
IF YOU PRACTICED MORE AND TALKED LESS, YOU'D FEEL AS ONE WITH THE TRIBE.

YOU'D NEVER REPEAT THE SELFISH ERRORS THAT CAUSE US ALL TROUBLE.
DUTY, DUTY, DUTY!
C'MON, ARROW-HEAD! YOU KNOW YOU LOVE ME!
sigh...

OF COURSE YOU'RE LOVED! BUT YOU COULD BE BETTER RESPECTED ...
...IF YOU TRULY WANTED TO.

SHORTLY...
WELL, LIFEMATE, GET YOUR TAIL TUCKED UNDER FOR YOU?
......

WYL...?
AFTER ALL THEIR SEASONS WITH US, MY EYRN...
...I FEAR THESE GO-BACKS WILL NEVER TAKE "THE WAY" SERIOUSLY!

HMPH! ALWAYS LOCK-SENDING ...FULL OF SECRETS!
BECAUSE WE CAN'T TRUST YOU TO PUT THE TRIBE'S GOOD FIRST!
UH OH!

THAT DOES IT!
YOU HIDE-BOUND ELDERS THINK YOU'RE BETTER THAN US!
THINK YOU'RE HIGH ONES!
WHOA, SKOT! THEY MIGHT AS WELL BE!

SO WHAT?! GO-BACKS TREAT EVERYONE THE SAME!
HE MEANS WE DON'T GROW OLD, IF WE CAN HELP IT--
--SO WE DON'T LEARN TO RESPECT AGE!

AT LEAST WE CAN LAUGH WITH TREESTUMP AND CLEAR-BROOK!
BUT A FERN LAUGHS MORE THAN STRONG-BOW!
AND NEITHER OF YOU SHARE!
THERE'S NO GETTING CLOSE TO YOU!
IS THAT WHAT YOU THINK?

SIT!
???

OOOHH...!
NNNH...!

T-TOO STRONG!
IT HURTS!
WE KNOW

BUT ***THIS*** IS WHAT YOU WANT.
WORDS AREN'T ENOUGH.
BODIES AREN'T ENOUGH.
THIS IS HOW ***WE*** SHARE.

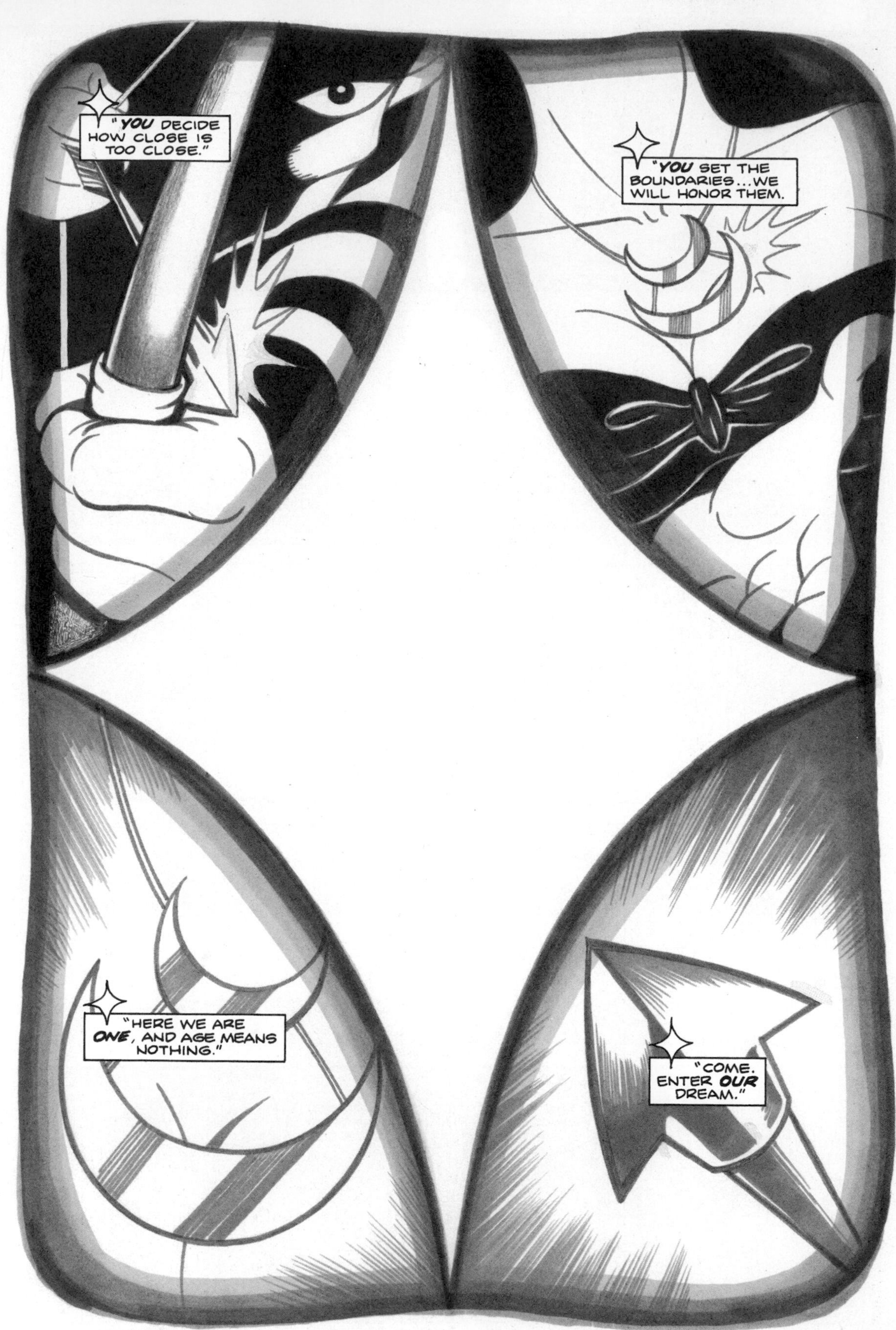
"YOU DECIDE HOW CLOSE IS TOO CLOSE."
"YOU SET THE BOUNDARIES... WE WILL HONOR THEM.
"HERE WE ARE ONE, AND AGE MEANS NOTHING."
"COME. ENTER OUR DREAM."

ENOUGH! N-NO DEEPER!
WHY-WHY GIVE SO MUCH OF YOURSELVES ...TO US?
FROM ANYONE WHO INVITES US...OR IS INVITED--

--WE WITHHOLD NOTHING BUT OUR SOUL NAMES.
whew! AND I THOUGHT...

...THAT OUR HEADS, OUR HEARTS, OUR RULES WERE SMALL --
--AND THAT STANDING OVER YOU MADE US FEEL BIG?
WE...OUR WOLF-FRIENDS... WE'RE ALL JUST BITS OF FLESH, SWIRLING IN A VASTDEEP SEA WHERE ALL IS POSSIBLE!
NOTHING EVER GETS DONE -NOTHING CAN- UNLESS WE ABIDE BY THE RULES WE MAKE.

OUR TRIBE ENDURES, EACH OF US KNOWING OUR PART.
WHERE DO YOU STAND?

AND SO...
Hmmm...WHAT D'YOU THINK I'LL HAVE TO TRADE OLD PICKNOSE FOR A TWO-BLADED AXE, EH, CUTTER?
DUNNO, TREESTUMP. BETTER CATCH 'IM WHILE HE'S STILL SOFT AS NUT-MASH FROM GETTING TRINKET BACK.
GO ON, SILLY-- HE WON'T BITE YOU!
DON'T BE SO SURE, SHEN-SHEN!
HSSHT! SHUT UP, WILL YOU?

WELL...?

Heh Heh Heh...
...ALL RIGHT!
TAIL IT OUT OF HERE BEFORE I NIP YOUR GRINNING MUZZLE OFF!

NOW, WHY DON'T I EVER TRY THAT ON CUTTER?
YEEEHOOOO!!
OH, PIKE! COME OUT OF YOUR DREAMBERRY FOG!
SKOT PICKED THAT TRICK UP FROM YOU!

TYLEET! SHENSHEN! MY RUMP IS SAVED!!
giggle WONDERFUL! NOW, CAN YOU KEEP IT OUT OF TROUBLE?

THAT DEPENDS! UP FOR A LITTLE PLAY, LOVELY MAIDENS?
NOTHING SOUL-PIERCING! NOTHING DEEP! NO SKULL-ACHES!
WOOOOO! NO ARGUMENTS FROM ME!
chuckle

CUTTER HAS FORGIVEN, BUT THE TALL ONES WON'T FORGET.
THEY CAPTURED LEETAH DAYS AGO.
AND OTHERS SAW SKOT AND KRIM LAST NIGHT.

THEY KNOW WE'RE HERE.
BEFRIENDING THEM IS OUR BEST HOPE...
...AND MY FONDEST DREAM...

WOLFRIDERS **HUNT**, **HOWL**, **GUARD** AND **PLAY**. IN THEIR PREDATORY WORLD, NOTHING THEY CREATE IS EXPECTED TO LAST... NOTHING IS **MEANT** TO.
PIKE'S NOTION OF COLLECTING DREAMS TO FIND THE COMMON THREAD WHICH BINDS THEM IS STILL VERY NEW AND **STRANGE** TO HIS TRIBE.
PERHAPS I UNDERSTAND YOUR DREAM GAME BEST... BECAUSE I'VE BEEN CLOSER TO A HUMAN THAN ANY OF THE OTHERS.
AND HUMANS ALWAYS TRY TO **HANG ON** TO THINGS, EH, **TYLEET**?
HEH HEH! LEAVE IT TO **ME** TO TRY KEEPING WHAT NO HAND CAN HOLD!
DREAMTIME
WHEN IT COMES TO THE **TALL ONES**, MOST OF US WANT TO LIVE AND LET LIVE.
BUT I HOPE A TIME WILL COME WHEN WE LEARN FROM THEM-- HELP THEM--AND **THEY** DO AS MUCH FOR US!

IN MY DREAM, WORDS OPEN THE PATH TO FRIEND-SHIP.
THEY AREN'T ENOUGH. BUT THEY MAKE GOOD BEGINNINGS.
"I ALWAYS WONDERED WHAT MY CUBLING LITTLE PATCH DREAMT OF, FOR WE COULDN'T SEND TO EACH OTHER.
"IN THE SLEEP-VISION I RECALL BEST, HE WANDERS OUT OF THE WOODS INTO AN OPEN FIELD.
"BEYOND IT LIES A SETTLEMENT BUILT BY MANY HUMANS. IT LOOKS VERY ODD...
"...TALLER THAN SHENSHEN'S SENDING-PICTURES OF THE SUN VILLAGE'S HUTS.
"I DON'T WANT LITTLE PATCH TO GO THERE.
"TO BE SURE, THAT'S JUST WHAT HE DID WHEN HE WAS GROWN...
"...BUT IN MY DREAM, MY FEELINGS ARE ALL THOSE OF A SHE-WOLF PROTECTING A TINY CUB.
"I GIVE CHASE. BUT MY LEGS MOVE SO SLOWLY! IT'S AS IF I'M STRUGGLING AGAINST THE CURRENT OF A SWOLLEN STREAM!

"BEFORE I CAN REACH HIM, LITTLE PATCH HAS TODDLED ACROSS THE FIELD, RIGHT INTO THAT QUEER, BUSY PLACE FULL OF HUMANS.
"I LOSE HIM SO QUICKLY AMONGST THE TWO-LEGGED HERD.
"WHERE ARE THEY ALL GOING? WHAT ARE THEY ALL UP TO...
"...THAT THEY CAN'T STOP A MOMENT TO TEND A MOTHERLESS CUB?
"NEXT TO PATCH, I'M THE SMALLEST HERE. I SEE NOTHING BUT WIDE-STRIDING LEGS.
"HOW FRIGHTENING IT MUST BE FOR **HIM**!
"TO ALL MY CALLS, THERE IS NO ANSWERING CRY.

"THE TALL ONES NOTICE ME, IN MY SEARCH, AND STARE. THEY DON'T SEEM TO BE AFRAID.
"I DARE TO ASK FOR HELP. BUT THEY CAN'T UNDERSTAND ME.
"EVEN SO, THEY SENSE MY NEED.
"THE FIRST TO COME FORWARD ARE THE FRIENDLY ONES...
"...NONNA AND ADAR! FROM WHAT I'VE HEARD, I KNOW THEY'LL HELP FIND LITTLE PATCH.
"BUT, TO MY SURPRISE, THEIR WORDS ARE JUST GABBLE!
"I LISTEN CLOSELY, UNTIL THEIR MEANING SOMEHOW COMES CLEAR.
"THEN I TRY IMITATING THEIR STRANGE TALK.
"MY MOUTH SHAPES IT POORLY, AT FIRST.
"THEN THE WORDS TAKE FORM...BECOMING LOUDER, MORE SURE...
"AT LAST I'M ABLE TO SAY..."
I HAVE A HUMAN SON--LITTLE PATCH.
HE IS LOST AMONG YOU. WILL YOU HELP?

"SADLY, ONCE MY WORDS ARE UNDERSTOOD, MY DEEDS ARE NOT.
"WHEN THEY LEARN I'VE RAISED ONE OF THEIR KIND, SOME OF THEM ARE GREATLY OFFENDED.
"THEY DISTRUST ME AND TURN AWAY BECAUSE...
"...IN THE END, I'M NOT ONE OF THEM.
"I GO ON ALONE, CALLING IN HUMAN TONGUE."
LITTLE PATCH!
LITTLE PATCH!
COME BACK!
"THE HUMAN HERD IS BIG IN EVERY WAY, AND I AM VERY SMALL.
"THEY'VE SNATCHED MY CUB, I KNOW IT! THEY THINK HE BELONGS WITH THEM!"
NO...
...NOT YET!
NOT YET!
sob sob
"SOMEONE HUGE COMES UP BEHIND.
"AM I NOW TO PAY WITH MY FREEDOM, MERELY FOR ASKING THEIR HELP?

"NO! IT'S THE GRUFF, KINDLY ONE CUTTER HAS TOLD OF...
"...THAT GREAT BEAR OF A HUMAN, OLBAR, WHO LIFTS ME HIGH ABOVE THE HERD!
"NO ONE QUESTIONS, OR EVEN LOOKS SIDEWAYS AS WE PASS."
LITTLE PATCH! LITTLE PATCH!
WHERE ARE YOU, MY SON?!
"I LOOK OVER THE FLOCK OF BOBBING HEADS AND...
"I SEE I'M TRUSTED AFTER ALL!
"THEY'VE FOUND HIM! THEY'RE BRINGING HIM TO ME!
"WHY? WHAT HAS CHANGED?
"AS I CUDDLE MY PRECIOUS CUB, I SEE THE ANSWER AT ONCE...

"I *AM* ONE OF THEM! I HAVE *FIVE* FINGERS ON EACH HAND!
"THROUGH THIS DREAM-GIFT, I'VE LIVED THE NEED LITTLE PATCH MUST HAVE KNOWN ALL HIS LIFE..."
...THE NEED TO BE ACCEPTED.
MAYBE IT'S ONLY IN DREAMS THAT THINGS TURN OUT SO WELL.
OH, I DON'T KNOW...
WELL, SHENSHEN! DID YOU SHOW *SKOT* ANY NEW *ROMPS*?
THERE'S SOMETHING TO BE SAID FOR OLD FAVORITES! giggle
AS FOR THINGS TURNING OUT... IF I COULD MAKE FRIENDS, OF SORTS, WITH THAT GROUCHY *OLD MAGGOTY*...
...*ANYTHING* IS POSSIBLE!

DO YOU HAVE A DREAM-TALE ABOUT THAT LOVELY OLD MUD-GRUBBER?
Hmm. IN PART. BUT MOSTLY ABOUT LOVELY *ME*!
I REMEMBER IT SO WELL...

...BECAUSE IT'S THE LAST DREAM I HAD BEFORE THE TROLLS WOKE US.
AND FUNNIEST OF ALL...*YOU'RE* IN IT, TOO, TYLEET!
TELL ON!

"WELL, I'M BACK IN SORROW'S END. AND, AS USUAL, LEETAH OUTSHINES ME IN EVERY WAY.
"I PLAY THE SIDE-WATCHER CHEERFULLY, AS I ALWAYS DO.
"PART OF ME KNOWS SHE WILL DISAPPEAR SOON. THE SOONER THE BETTER!
"I'M WICKED! IT'S SHAMEFUL, I KNOW!
"BUT MY DREAM-SELF DOESN'T CARE HOW MUCH I'LL MISS HER!
"I HURRY TO SAVAH'S HUT...
"...AND ASK THE WISE MOTHER OF MEMORY..."
WHAT WILL MAKE ME SHINE BRIGHTER THAN LEETAH... EVEN JUST ONCE?

"SAVAH PROMISES TO SHOW ME SOMETHING.
"IT MAKES ME SO HAPPY! I ALWAYS DEPEND ON HER GUIDANCE!
"SHE LEADS ME DOWNSTAIRS TO HER PRIVATE, UNDERGROUND CHAMBER.
"BUT, OH MY! THE STAIRS TURN INTO A TUNNEL AND THE ELEGANT CHAMBER BECOMES A DANK, SMELLY CAVE.
"AND SAVAH... giggle THIS IS SO SILLY!
"SAVAH TURNS INTO OLD MAGGOTY!
"SHE GOES GAB-GAB-GABBING AWAY, JUST LIKE SHE ALWAYS DOES.
"I SAY I DON'T QUITE UNDERSTAND...
"...AND THAT MAKES HER VERY, VERY ANGRY!"
!!**??¢!!!

"SHE MAKES IT CLEAR MY TASK IS TO PICK CERTAIN ROOTS AND MUSHROOMS AND PLACE THEM IN HER BASKET.
"I GRUDGINGLY OBEY...
"...THOUGH IT'S PAST ME HOW THIS WILL HELP ME SHINE APART FROM MY SISTER!
"MY TROLL TEACHER CERTAINLY HAS SOME LESSON IN MIND, FOR EACH TIME I REACH TO PLUCK UP A TREASURE--
"A GREAT BOOT STOMPS DOWN AND CRUSHES IT!
"IT HAPPENS AGAIN--
"--AND AGAIN!

"AND THEN...IT ALMOST HAPPENS TO *ME*!
"BUT I 'WAKE UP' JUST IN TIME!"
¿cackle cackle¿ A DREAM WITHIN A DREAM!
"HMPH! WITH WHATEVER OLD MAGGOTY THINKS IS FUNNY, I SELDOM AGREE.
"THERE IS A THUNDEROUS RUMBLING ABOVE. THE CAVE WALLS SHUDDER AND START TO SQUEEZE IN!"
AM-- AM I DREAMING...? RIGHT NOW?
Hee Hee Heee! LITTLE DUNCE! DREAMS NEVER HAPPEN "NOW!"
"NOW *I'M* THE ANGRY ONE!"
NO MORE TRICKS! TELL ME HOW TO OUTSHINE LEETAH!
YOU'LL COME INTO YOUR OWN, PIGLET PIE!

" 'BUT NOT WHEN YOU THINK YOU OUGHT,' SHE SAYS."
WHEN?
THEN WHEN?
"OLD MAGGOTY JUST LAUGHS. THE CAVE IS DARK, STIFLING, CLOSING IN!
"CAN'T **BREATHE**! I MUST FLEE OR CHOKE!
"BUT THERE, ON THE GROUND BEFORE ME, LIES MY BEAUTIFUL SISTER! I **CAN'T** LEAVE HER!"
OH, LEETAH! I'M DREAMING IN A DARK CAVE, BECAUSE OF **YOU**!
WHEN WILL I SEE **MY OWN** LIGHT?!
"NOW THIS YOU'LL LIKE! LEETAH TURNS OVER AND...
"...SHE'S **YOU**, TYLEET! AND YOU SAY..."
SHINE-- WHERE YOU **LOVE**!
"THEN YOU SHOW ME YOU ARE WITH CUB! YOU HOLD OUT YOUR HAND AND...
"...IT HAS **FIVE FINGERS**!"

AND...?
AND THAT'S ALL. THAT'S WHEN THE TROLLS SLICED OPEN MY COCOON!
MY FIVE FINGERS... IN YOUR DREAM TOO.
WE MUST HAVE TOUCHED THOUGHTS AS WE SLEPT!

OH, I HOPE YOUR VISION OF ME WITH CUB COMES TRUE!
TO ME IT FEELS AS IF IT ALREADY HAS!
OH, PUCKER-NUTS!

I GET IT!
I SEE!
TYLEET!
SHENSHEN!
THANK-YOUTHANK-YOUTHANK-YOU!
WHOOSH!
???
CUTTER! I FOUND IT!
I FOUND THE THREAD!

YOU HAVE TO CALL COUNCIL NOW!
HUH?
WHAT'S UP, PIKE?

THE DREAM GAME! IT'S ALMOST DONE, CUTTER! I'LL EXPLAIN--
--SOON AS YOU, AROREE AND CLEARBROOK HAVE TOLD YOURS!
BEFORE THE ENTIRE TRIBE?! BAT DUNG!

YOU'RE NOT GETTING **ME** TO--
--EH?

TIMMAIN! YOU **WANT** US TO SEE THIS FOOLISHNESS THROUGH?
Whuff!
ALL RIGHT! I **KNOW** THAT LOOK!

"LET'S GET IT OVER WITH!"

SILENTLY, ONE BY ONE, **CUTTER** STUDIES EACH FACE IN THE **COUNCIL** OF **WOLFRIDERS**.
HIS EYES LINGER LONGEST ON THE FEATURES OF HIS LIFEMATE, CHILDREN AND BROTHER... THE FAMILY **SO LONG LOST** TO HIM AND, INCREDIBLY, **HIS** ONCE MORE.
IT WAS NOT CUTTER'S WISH TO CALL THE TRIBE TOGETHER THIS NIGHT. SAVE FOR THE PROMPTINGS OF **TIMMAIN**, THE **HIGH ONE** IN WOLF GUISE, HE WOULD **NOT** HAVE DONE SO.
NOT, AT LEAST, FOR THE REASON **PIKE** NOW VOICES.
FOR DAYS, NOW, I'VE BEEN GATHERING YOUR **DREAMS** LIKE SEEDS...
DREAMTIME PART 10
...AND IT HASN'T BEEN THE **SIMPLEST** TASK, I CAN TELL YOU!

SOME OF YOU "PODS" HAVE BEEN HARDER TO PRY OPEN THAN OTHERS!
gr-r-r-umble
AND SOME "POD PAIRS" HAVE SHARED BUT ONE SEED BETWEEN THEM!
SKOT SPOKE FOR ME, LIFEMATE, THAT'S SURE!

...BUT THE HIGH ONE HERSELF WANTS THE GATHERING FINISHED.
SO I'VE ASKED THAT WE DO IT HERE, IN COUNCIL, TONIGHT.

TYLEET AND SHENSHEN LIT UP MY HEAD. THEY GAVE ME THE COMMON THREAD...
...THAT BINDS MY BAG OF DREAM-SEEDS TOGETHER. AT LEAST, I THINK THEY DID.

BUT BEFORE I TRY UNTYING IT FOR US ALL...
...CLEAR-BROOK, AROREE AND CUTTER MUST BE HEARD.

"THEY'RE THE LAST THREE SEEDS MISSING FROM MY BAG...
"...AND FOR ALL I KNOW, THE MOST IMPORTANT ONES!"

MY DREAMS HAVE ALWAYS BEEN SIMPLE, PIKE. UNTIL NOW, I'VE NEVER GIVEN THEM MUCH THOUGHT.
IN THEM I RELIVE HUNTS AND HOWLS...

...AND SMALL PLEASURES WITH MY LIFEMATE -- THE STUFF OF EVERY DAY.
IT WAS NO DIFFERENT DURING THE LONG SLEEP. EXCEPT...

EXCEPT...?
I RECALL HAVING ONE DREAM WHEREIN I KNEW I DREAMED...
...AND WISHED WITH ALL MY BEING THAT I COULD WAKE!

"IT TOOK ME BACK TO THE DAYS JUST AFTER THE ***FIRST WAR*** FOR THE PALACE. DAYS THAT HELD SOME PEACE..."

"...BUT MORE OFTEN ***CONFUSION***, AS WE TRIED TO REMAKE OUR LIVES IN THE FORBIDDEN GROVE.

"WITH OUR FINDING OF THE PALACE, OUR KNOWING OF THE WORLD AND OUR PLACE IN IT WAS ALL ***UNSETTLED***.

"AGAINST ***THE WAY***, WE LIVED IN FEAR... FEAR OF SENDING... FEAR OF HAVING OUR VERY ***SOULS*** SNATCHED BY THE ***BLACK SNAKE***.

"DOES ANYONE REMEMBER?"

I DO. AFTER THE WAR IT SEEMED, FOR A TIME, THE WAY WENT DIM BEFORE ME.
THE MORE I TRIED TO THINK AND PLAN US ALL OUT OF TROUBLE, THE MORE TANGLED EVERYTHING GOT.
IN THE END, GUESSES AND LUCK WERE ALL I COULD COUNT ON.
AYE. IT WASN'T THE CLEAREST OF TIMES FOR ANY OF US.
DREAMS AREN'T ALWAYS KIND. SOMETIMES THEY MAKE US RELIVE MOMENTS WE'D JUST AS SOON FORGET.
OR MAKE US SEE THINGS WE HOPE WE'LL NEVER LIVE TO SEE!
"BLUE MOUNTAIN WAS A TWISTED, UNNATURAL PLACE, TO BE SURE. BUT IN MY DREAM, IT'S EVEN MORESO."
"I'M DEEP INSIDE, SEARCHING FOR WINDKIN.
"THE KIDNAPPED CUB IS HELD CAPTIVE SOMEWHERE IN THIS DISEASED STRONGHOLD."

"THOUGH I'VE BEEN HERE BEFORE, I DON'T KNOW MY WAY ABOUT. THERE IS NO SCENT TRAIL TO FOLLOW.
"IT MADDENS ME THAT I **DARE** NOT SEND TO THE CUB, BECAUSE THE BLACK SNAKE MIGHT CATCH MY THOUGHTS... AND ME.
"I TRAVEL THROUGH NARROW PASSAGEWAYS, **LOST** AND FULL OF FEAR.
"MY HEART POUNDS IN MY THROAT. I PANT **HARD**, UNABLE TO CATCH MY BREATH.
"THE STONE WALLS ARE DARK AND COVERED WITH RAISED SYMBOLS.
"THEY COME TO LIFE AND **THREATEN**!
"BUT I MOVE PAST THEM AND CONTINUE THE SEARCH FOR THE CUB.

"ENEMIES MADE OF FLESH LURK HERE TOO... WINNOWILL'S CHOSEN EIGHT.
"AT EVERY TURN I AM BRACED FOR THEIR ATTACK.
"THERE! AHEAD! SOMETHING MOVES IN THE DARKNESS!
"THAT FAMILIAR SCENT! WHO IS IT?
"TWO-EDGE!
"HE WANTS TO SPEAK...
AAARRGGHH!
SPLUTCH!
"...BUT I GIVE HIM NO CHANCE.

"AFIRE WITH RAGE AND FEAR COMBINED, I PLUNGE ONWARD.
"THE LITTLE CUB'S HOWLING! IT GUIDES ME!
"AROUND THE NEXT BEND...
"...I COME UPON THE BLACK SNAKE HERSELF!"
Heh Heh Heh Heh Heh
WAAAH! AAWAAAA!
"SHE CLUTCHES WINDKIN IN HER COILS! I KNOW WHAT HER POISON CAN DO TO ME...
"...TO HIM
"BUT MY DREAM-SELF HAS NO WISDOM.
"THE FURY BLAZING WITHIN MY HEART CAN BE QUENCHED ONLY BY HER BLOOD!
"gasp! AGAIN, TWO-EDGE!
"AGAIN HE WOULD HAVE WORDS!
"AGAIN I CUT HIM DOWN BEFORE HE CAN UTTER THEM!"
GAAAAAH!
FWAASHH!

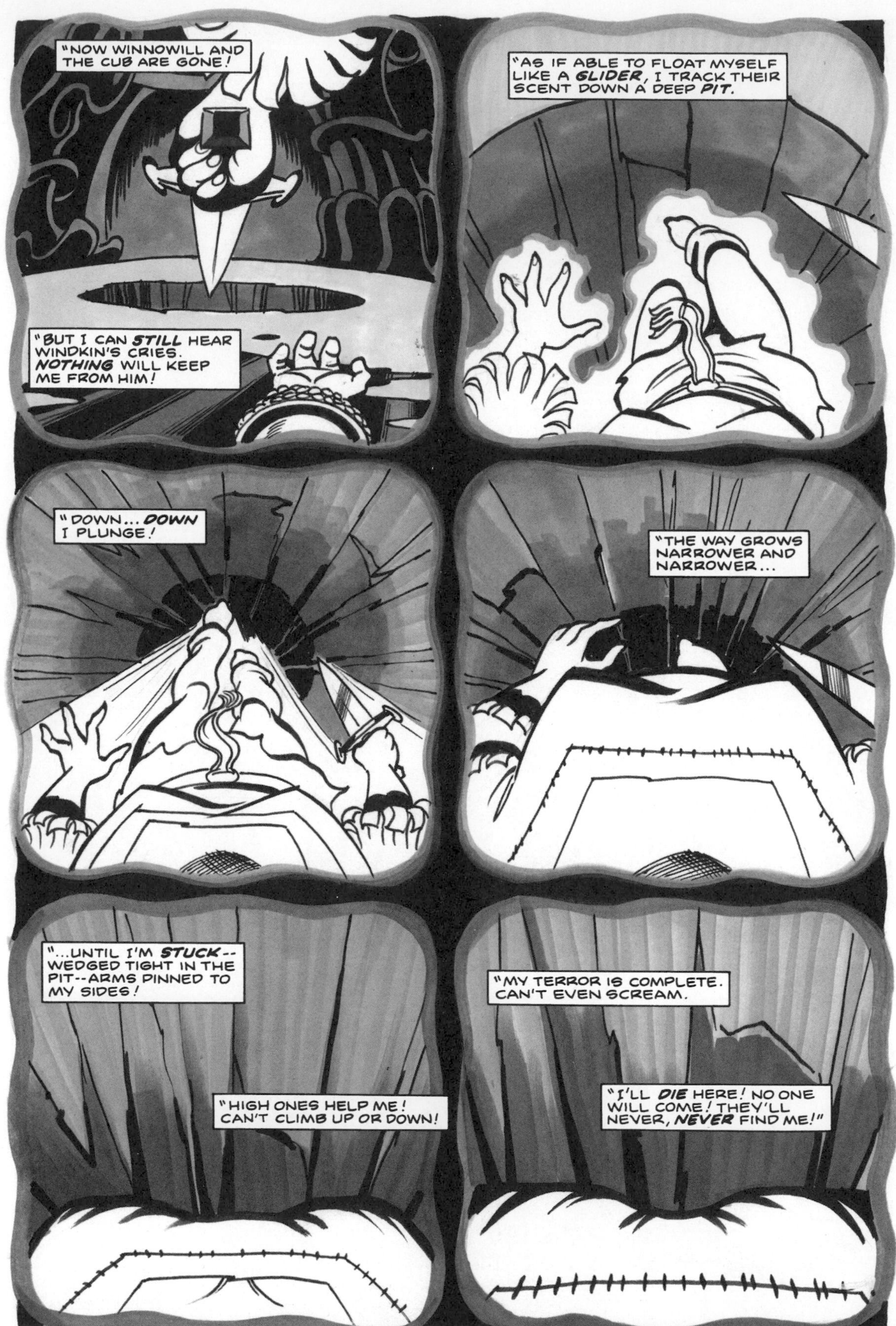
"NOW WINNOWILL AND THE CUB ARE GONE!
"BUT I CAN STILL HEAR WINDKIN'S CRIES. NOTHING WILL KEEP ME FROM HIM!
"AS IF ABLE TO FLOAT MYSELF LIKE A GLIDER, I TRACK THEIR SCENT DOWN A DEEP PIT.
"DOWN... DOWN I PLUNGE!
"THE WAY GROWS NARROWER AND NARROWER...
"...UNTIL I'M STUCK-- WEDGED TIGHT IN THE PIT--ARMS PINNED TO MY SIDES!
"HIGH ONES HELP ME! CAN'T CLIMB UP OR DOWN!
"MY TERROR IS COMPLETE. CAN'T EVEN SCREAM.
"I'LL DIE HERE! NO ONE WILL COME! THEY'LL NEVER, NEVER FIND ME!"

"AND THEN..."
RAP! RAP!
KRAK KRAK-KRAK-KRAK!
"...THE WALL BEFORE ME SHATTERS."
K-K-KRUMMBLE!
"TWO-EDGE, ALIVE AND WHOLE DESPITE MY BEST THRUSTS, WORKS TO RELEASE ME!
"'BUT-BUT I KILLED YOU,' I SAY."
NO. YOU DIDN'T.
"IT'S TRUE! NOW I KNOW THAT I AM DREAMING!
"'THEN WINDKIN IS ALREADY SAFE,' I SAY."
NO. HE IS NOT.
CHILDREN ARE NEVER SAFE.
NONE OF US EVER ARE...
NONE OF US...
NONE OF US...
NONE OF US...

THAT'S ALL.
WHOOF!
LIKE-- BUT NOT LIKE --WHAT REALLY HAPPENED!
TWO-EDGE DID SAVE YOU AND WINDKIN!

BUT MY TRUE ACTIONS, THANK THE HIGH ONES, WEREN'T SO RASH AS THOSE OF MY DREAM-SELF.
I HOPE I WENT ON TO SOME OTHER, CALMER VISION.

YOU DID!
AROREE! YOU SHARED A DREAM WITH CLEARBROOK?

SHARED?
NO...
...VISITED!
IF EVER I HAD A DREAM OF MY OWN...

...IT HAPPENED TOO LONG AGO FOR ME TO RECALL, MUCH LESS TELL OF IT!
LOVE-MATE...?

WHY DO YOU SEEM SO... ASHAMED?
YOUR TRIBE TOOK ME IN, SKYWISE...
...TRUSTED ME AS ONE OF THEM. NOW THEY MUST LEARN WHAT I DID AS I SLEPT THE LONG SLEEP...
...THOUGH IT COSTS ME THAT TRUST FOREVER!

IT FROZE MY BLOOD TO LEARN, UPON WAKING, THAT LORD WINNOWILL STILL LIVES.
SHE IS NOT THE ONLY ONE WHO FEEDS ON DREAMS.
"SHE TAUGHT THAT TRICK TO HER CHOSEN EIGHT AS WELL...
"...TAUGHT US TO VISIT OTHERS' SLEEPING MINDS IN SUBTLE, SECRET WAYS...UNDETECTABLE!
"BUT THE COST WAS HIGH--TERRIBLY HIGH!
"IN TIME, WE LOST THE ABILITY TO DREAM FOR OURSELVES.
"THE EMPTINESS--UNBEARABLE! IT SET US ALL A FEATHER'S BREADTH AWAY FROM MADNESS!"

MY LITTLE LOVE, YOU CANNOT KNOW WHAT IT IS TO LAY YOUR HEAD DOWN...
...AND SLIP INTO A NOTHINGNESS BLACKER THAN DEATH!

TO BE AWARE THAT, BECAUSE YOU ARE NOT DEAD, YOU SHOULD BE DREAMING... BUT CAN'T!
IT'S WRONG TO ENTER OTHERS' THOUGHTS UNASKED.

THAT'S WHY, IN OUR BRIEF TIME TOGETHER, YOU NEVER SAW ME SLEEP.
AND IN ALL YOUR SEASONS HERE ON THORNY MOUNTAIN, YOU NEVER SLEPT EITHER?!

HIGH ONES! HOW BRAVE YOU WERE TO LET YOURSELF BE COCOONED WITH THE REST!
!!!
BRAVE INDEED... CONSIDERING!

DEAR TRIBEMATES! YOU DON'T ABHOR MY SECRET VISITATIONS, THEN?
THEY WERE ONLY FOR COMFORT, AROREE.
HOLD IT!

YOU MEAN I'VE SPENT DAYS WHEEDLING SLEEP VISIONS--
--OUT OF THE SURLIEST OF THIS BUNCH, WHILE ALL THE TIME YOU--?!

OH, PIKE! EVERY DREAM THAT'S BEEN TOLD SINCE YOUR GAME BEGAN...
...I HAVE KNOWN IN DETAIL ALREADY!

AND MORE BESIDES.
THEN... YOU UNDERSTAND.

ALL TOO WELL, MY CHIEF.
HMPH! AND I THOUGHT I'D IMPRESS EVERYONE BY UNTYING MY BAG OF DREAM-SEEDS TONIGHT!
BUT IT'S AROREE AND CUTTER WHO'VE HELD THE COMMON THREAD ALL ALONG!
MAKE NO MISTAKE. YOUR DREAM-GAME HAS SERVED A GOOD PURPOSE, PIKE.

IT'S MADE US A CLOSE-KNIT PACK AGAIN...

HELPED US EACH TO RELEARN OUR PLACE AND OUR DUTIES.

BUT MY ADVICE AS CHIEF IS...

...LET THE GAME END **NOW**!

OUR ONLY TASK, IN THIS NEW TIME, IS TO BE WHAT WE ARE... **WOLFRIDERS**!

TO LIVE **THE WAY**, NO MATTER HOW MUCH THE FOREST, THE LAND AND EVEN THE **ENTIRE WORLD** HAVE CHANGED!

CUT THE THREAD, PIKE! SCATTER YOUR DREAM-SEEDS AND LET THEM GROW WILD!
THEY'LL BEAR BLOSSOMS OR THORNS IN THEIR OWN TIME. DON'T RUSH THINGS.
CUTTER...

"WHAT'S YOUR DREAM?"
......

UUH... UM, HEY!
SNAP!
DON'T I GET A TURN?

ALL THE DREAMS HAVE NOW BEEN TOLD, ONE APIECE, BY THOSE WHO SLEPT THE LONG SLEEP IN THE NEW LAND...
...ALL, THAT IS, SAVE CUTTER'S. TO HIS GREAT RELIEF, HIS MOMENT MUST WAIT AS...
BUT--BUT YOU WEREN'T COCOONED WITH THE REST OF US, SKYWISE!
SO? YOU WON'T KNOW IF MY DREAM FITS IN OR NOT 'TIL YOU HEAR IT!
HE'S RIGHT! REMEMBER, IN MY SLEEP-VISION OLD MAGGOTY SAID DREAMS NEVER HAPPEN "NOW."
DREAMTIME
PART 11
SEEMS TO ME THEY'RE ALL FOR FUN, SHENSHEN...A WAY FOR OUR SPIRITS TO PLAY WHILE OUR BODIES REST!

OH YOU DO, DO YOU?
Hmph! YOU THINK MY DREAM... OR NIGHTFALL'S... WERE "FUN," CUB?
SCARY FUN, TREE-STUMP...
...BECAUSE THEY NEVER HAPPENED, ANY MORE THAN THE ONE I HAD YESTERDAY DID!
I ONLY WISH IT COULD! LISTEN...
"IT'S NIGHT. I'M ALL ALONE ON A HILLTOP, GUARDING A CART. DUNNO WHY.
"IT'S FULL OF TREASURE -- PIECES OF GOLD! -- ALL TIED IN NEAT BUNDLES AND STACKED IN A BIG PILE.
"THERE'S AN EXTRA BAG I KNOW IS MINE!
"HEH HEH... I MAKE SURE IT DOESN'T GET MIXED IN WITH THE BIG TREASURE!

"SUDDENLY I HEAR HOOFBEATS! HUMANS... RIDING NOHUMPS!
"THEY'RE SEARCHING FOR THE CART, THE TREASURE... AND ME!

"SOMEHOW, I KNOW I'M TO TAKE THE TREASURE AND HIDE IT IN THE WOODS AT THE FOOT OF THE HILL.
"DON'T ASK HOW I LUG IT ALL DOWN THERE IN ONE TRIP! IT'S ENOUGH THAT I DO.

"FROM MY HIDING PLACE I CAN SEE THE HILL AND THE DARK NIGHT SKY ABOVE--IT'S ALL SO CLEAR.
"THE NOHUMP RIDERS APPROACH THE EMPTY CART AND LOOK IT OVER.
"PUCKERNUTS! I'M JUST MOMENTS AWAY FROM BIG, BIG TROUBLE!

"BUT NO! THE HUMANS DON'T SEEM INTERESTED AFTER ALL! THEY LEAVE...

"...AND THEN, RIGHT OVER THE CART, HIGHER UP IN THE SKY THAN I HAVE WORDS TO TELL, THERE APPEARS A BUNCH OF VERY STRANGE STARS...
"...SO BIG, SO BRIGHT, THEY DON'T SEEM REAL!

"THEY START TO SWIRL ABOUT, EIGHTS UPON EIGHTS OF THEM...
"...LOOPING AND SWOOPING LIKE A FLOCK OF BIRDS... OR LIKE WINDBLOWN, COLORED LEAVES IN THE SEASON OF DEATH-SLEEP!
"SUDDENLY IT DAWNS ON ME-- THEY'RE ALIVE! AND THEY CAN THINK!
"I SENSE THEY'VE COME TO TAKE SOMETHING FROM HERE... TO SOME 'WHERE' ELSE.
"WHEREVER IT IS, I WANT TO GO TOO-- SO BADLY IT HURTS!
"OH, PLEASE... PLEASE... LET ME BE THE SOMETHING THEY MEAN TO CARRY AWAY!

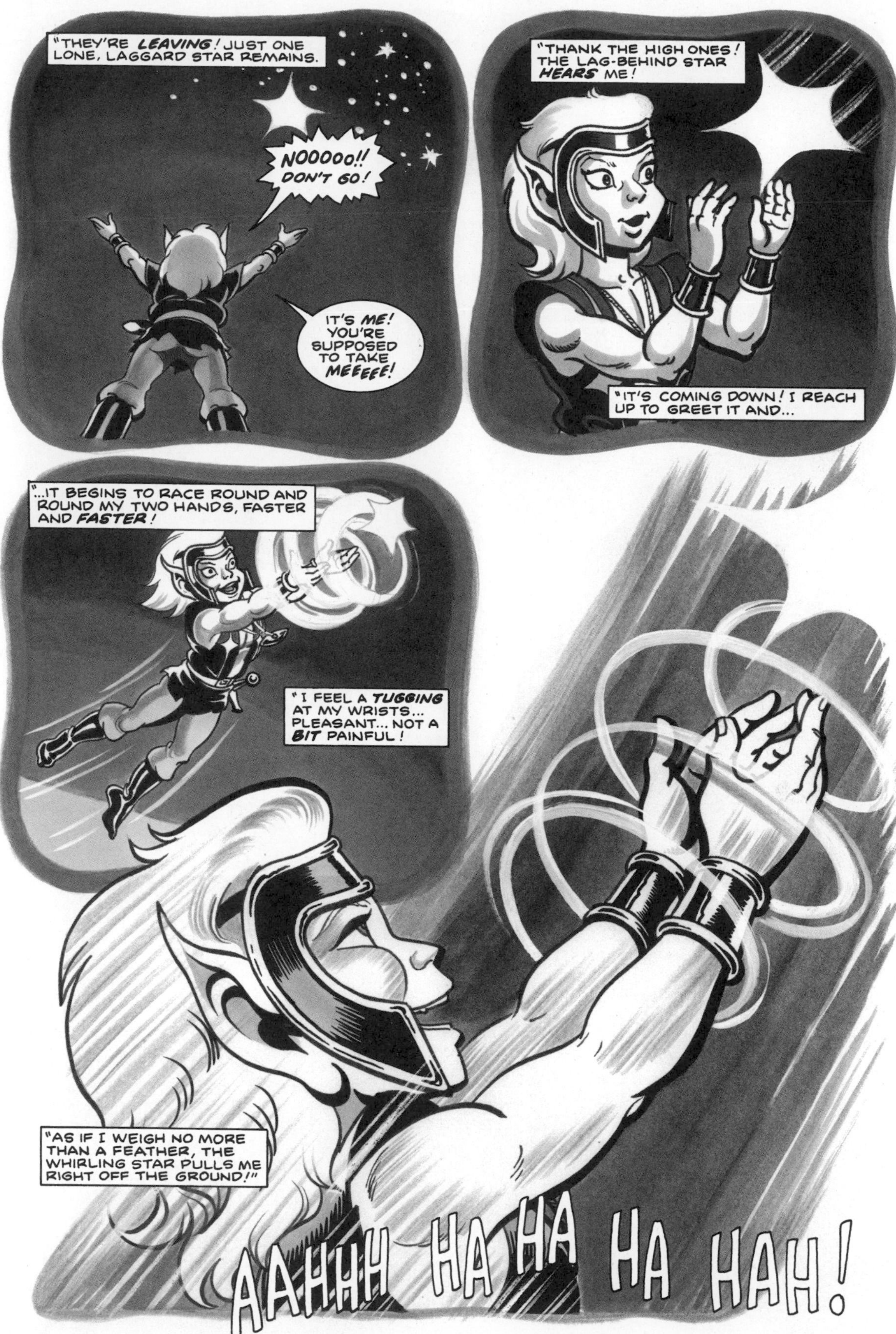
"THEY'RE LEAVING! JUST ONE LONE, LAGGARD STAR REMAINS.
NOOOOO!! DON'T GO!
IT'S ME! YOU'RE SUPPOSED TO TAKE MEEEEEE!
"THANK THE HIGH ONES! THE LAG-BEHIND STAR HEARS ME!
"IT'S COMING DOWN! I REACH UP TO GREET IT AND...
"...IT BEGINS TO RACE ROUND AND ROUND MY TWO HANDS, FASTER AND FASTER!
"I FEEL A TUGGING AT MY WRISTS... PLEASANT... NOT A BIT PAINFUL!
"AS IF I WEIGH NO MORE THAN A FEATHER, THE WHIRLING STAR PULLS ME RIGHT OFF THE GROUND!"
AAHHH HA HA HA HAH!

"OH! HOW CAN I TELL OF THE JOY BUBBLING OUT OF ME AS I FLOAT UP, OVER THE HILLS... OVER THE WOODS... OVER THE HUMANS' HUTS?!
"FREE, THAT'S HOW I FEEL! FLOWN HIGH AND FAR BY A FRIENDLY STAR...
"...I WHOOP AND SHRIEK AND LAUGH OUT LOUD LIKE I'M COMPLETELY CRAZY!

"SUDDENLY, IT'S DAYTIME. I FLY, UNAFRAID, RIGHT DOWN TO THE HUMANS' BUSTLING HIVE.
"THEY SEE ME. AND I WANT THEM TO!
"I HAVE GREAT FUN SURPRISING THEM, WALKING ABOUT FOR A BIT...
"...THEN WISHING TO SOAR AWAY-- AND DOING IT...
"...AS EASILY AS A TUFTED SEEDLING RIDES THE BREEZE.
"I'M FREE... FREE TO CONQUER THE HIGHEST, CLOUD-TOUCHING ROOFTOP THE FIVE-FINGERED ONES, IN ALL OF THEIR PRIDE, HAVE BUILT.
"THEN, ALL AT ONCE, THE FLIGHT IS OVER.

"I FIND MYSELF IN A ROOM, SITTING ON THE SOFT CUSHIONS OF A SLEEPING-PIT!
"MY FRIENDLY STAR SHATTERS, SPRINKLING DOWN ON ME AS A BLANKET OF MAGIC...
"...THAT LOOKS JUST LIKE A PLAIN, OLD, RUSTY-COLORED HIDE!

"I TALK TO IT... CHATTERING ABOUT ALL THE CHANGES IN THE WORLD... AND IN ME. ABOUT GIVING UP MY WOLF BLOOD...
"...ABOUT BELIEVING MY WHOLE TRIBE DEAD, ONLY TO FIND THEM-- AND MY CHIEF-FRIEND-- SO MANY TURNS OLDER THAN I REMEMBER.

TELL ME, BLANKET... WHERE DO I BELONG?
"I GUESS IT'S THE RIGHT QUESTION...

"...BECAUSE IT GETS ME A MOST SURPRISING RESPONSE!

"IN HER BEAUTY SHE SHIMMERS LIKE THE STAR SHE ONCE WAS.
"AND THOUGH SHE SEEMS YOUNG, THERE'S A SENSE OF GREAT AGE AND WISDOM ABOUT HER.

"WE'RE BOTH DELIGHTED TO DISCOVER EACH OTHER.

"WILL SHE ANSWER MY QUESTION?
"WHAT?! MORE MAGIC!
"IT-IT'S STARJUMPER...!
"...LOOKING AT ME WITH HIS BRIGHT, BLACK EYES...
"...WANTING TO PLAY ROUGH-AND-TUMBLE LIKE HE ALWAYS DID!
"HE'S NOT THE ANSWER I WAS EXPECTING. BUT MAYBE..."

...MAYBE YOU'RE SUPPOSED TO LOOK *TWICE*!
MAYBE!
DREAMING OR AWAKE, *YOU'RE* AS I REMEMBER YOU, BROTHER...
...ALWAYS SOFTENING THE PATH FOR ME WITH A SMILE-- AND A DREAMBERRY-HEAD TALE.
CUTTER, YOU DON'T HAVE TO...
NO. PIKE'S RIGHT.
THE GAME WILL END HOW IT ENDS...WITH *ME*.

CUTTER'S SO CHANGED... LOOKS LIKE A HARDENED WARRIOR.
HOW CAN HE BE SO SCARED TO SHARE HIS DREAM... NO MATTER HOW BAD IT MAY BE ?
YOU ARE MY STRENGTH... ALWAYS WERE. I'VE NEVER NEEDED IT MORE!
LIFEMATE...
THIS GAME HASN'T BEEN MUCH FUN FOR SOME.
GUESS I'M GLAD IT'S ALMOST OVER.
DREAMTIME Pt 12
SQUARING HIS SHOULDERS, THE WOLFRIDER CHIEF SENDS...
...AN OPEN SENDING TO THE ENTIRE TRIBE.

"I'M ON THE BRIDGE OF DESTINY.
"IN PLACE OF THE SUN SYMBOL, MY GOAL IS LEETAH.
"SHE'S FAR AWAY... ON THE OTHER SIDE.
"THERE'S NOTHING BELOW ME...NO ROCKS, NO SUN VILLAGE...
"NOTHING BUT A BOTTOMLESS CHASM!
"I'M FROZEN TO THE SPOT... CAN'T MOVE!

"THEN, WITHOUT WARNING, HE SWEEPS HER OFF THE BRIDGE!
"MY RIVAL... MY GREAT ENEMY... RAYEK!
"I FALL, KNOWING I'VE FAILED HER-- FAILED EVERYONE!
"I'VE LOST THE TRIAL OF HEAD, HAND AND HEART!
"AND I'VE LOST SOMETHING ELSE... SOMETHING I'LL NEVER GET BACK..."
UNEXPECTEDLY, PAINFULLY, CUTTER BREAKS OFF THE SENDING...
HUH?!
ENOUGH! I'LL TAKE YOU NO FURTHER!
BELOVED...!
BUT YOUR DREAM'S NO WORSE THAN THE OTHERS, CUTTER! WHY--?
SORRY, PIKE!
IT'S NOT THE DREAM I FEAR TO SHARE...

IT'S WHAT FOLLOWS... THE COUNTING!
WHEN I FOUND MY FAMILY, I THOUGHT I'D BE HAPPY AGAIN. DIDN'T KNOW THE SADNESS WOULD STAY.
TIMMORN'S BLOOD! WHAT CAN WE DO?
LEETAH, THE CUBS AND I... WE'D GIVE ANYTHING TO MAKE IT LIKE IT WAS...
...BEFORE RAYEK...
YOU KNOW WHAT WILL HEAL YOUR HEART, BELOVED. PLEASE TELL!
THE "NOW OF WOLF THOUGHT..."
BUT IF I SEND HOW IT FEELS TO LOSE IT, THE TRIBE WILL LOSE IT TOO--
--AND THAT'LL BE THE END OF US! I'D RATHER DIE!
BUT-- BUT I...
DON'T PRESS HIM, PIKE.
DON'T SEEK A NAME FOR WHAT YOU HAVE.
IT'S TOO PRECIOUS.
THERE'S ONE ADVANTAGE. IN EXCHANGE FOR THE "NOW," I'VE GOTTEN GOOD AT LOOKING AHEAD.
AS CHIEF IN THESE NEW TIMES, IT'S A SKILL I'LL NEED PLENTY OF!
HOW DO YOU KNOW...?
HEH...
HAVEN'T YOU BEEN FOLLOWING THE DREAM GAME, YOUNGER BROTHER?

AHA!
I THOUGHT SO!
YOUR TALK ABOUT DREAMS MEANING NOTHING WAS ONLY THAT--TALK!
I KNEW IT ALL THE TIME!
SOMEHOW, WHILE WE SLEPT, THE WHOLE TRIBE CAUGHT THE SCENT OF WHAT LIES ON THE PATH BEFORE US.
SHOW HIM, PIKE.
SHOW US ALL WHAT YOU'VE FIGURED OUT!
HAH! FOR WHAT THAT'S WORTH--!
--PIKE'S ARROWS ARE MOSTLY HALF-COCKED!
BUT MY SPEAR MOSTLY HITS HOME! JUST WATCH!
AROREE... IF YOU PLEASE!
HEY! WHAT GIVES?
SPLITTING US UP...!?
I DON'T LIKE THIS!
WHAT'RE YOU TWO UP TO?
WHAT'S THE BIG IDEA, SPEAR-TOSSER?
SHENSHEN... TYLEET... YOU FIRST!
YOUR SHARED DREAM IS THE KEY TO ALL THE OTHERS!

I HOPE YOUR VISION OF ME WITH CUB COMES TRUE!
TO ME, IT SEEMS AS IF IT ALREADY HAS!
"ALREADY HAS!" THINK!
WHAT IF, WHEN WE'RE DREAMING, WE'RE REALLY LIVING AND DOING SOMEWHERE ELSE?
"IN HER SLEEP-VISION, TYLEET IS ACCEPTED BY HUMANS--AS HUMAN.
"WHEN THINGS START TO CLOSE IN ON HER, SHE'S HELPED BY THEM...LIFTED HIGH TO SEE FAR.
"WHO'S TO SAY THAT ISN'T ALREADY SO...OR WON'T BE?
"THINK OF OLD MAGGOTY'S WORDS IN SHENSHEN'S DREAM..."
cackle cackle DREAMS NEVER HAPPEN "NOW!"
"SHENSHEN AND TYLEET SHARE A KNOWING! 'NOW' MEANS 'HERE AND NOW!'"

"HERE"... THAT'S THE WORLD WHEN WE'RE AWAKE!
"NOW" IS ALL THERE IS WHEN WE'RE AWAKE!
AND WHAT'S BEFORE AND WHAT'S BEHIND ARE ALL ONE, RIGHT, LIFEMATES? THESE ARE VISIONS OF LIGHT!

Hmph! MY DREAM DIDN'T SEEM SO "LIGHT" TO ME!
WERE YOU SCARED?
NOT A BIT!
THAT'S WHAT I MEAN!

"LIGHT VISIONS HAVE NO FEAR IN THEM. OH, THINGS HAPPEN...

"LIKE SO-- ZHANTEE SEES THE SUN VILLAGE WIPED OUT.

"BUT HE GOES WITH IT AND IS RAISED HIGH, LIKE TYLEET, TO SEE FAR!

"SAME WITH VENKA. SHE FLIES ABOVE THE FIRE AND ICE WARRING FOR HER LOYALTY.

"BUT SHE LIFTS HERSELF!

"AND DO WE NEED TO TALK ABOUT SKYWISE'S DREAM?!"
EEEEYOOWW! HOO HOOO HA HAHA
chuckle
WHAT ABOUT YOURS? WHEN YOUR SURROUNDINGS CLOSED IN ON YOU--
"--YOU DIDN'T EXACTLY RISE ABOVE 'EM!"
NOPE... BUT I WASN'T SCARED!
FLYING HIGH OR CREEPING LOW, YOU STILL SEE FARTHER THAN WHEN YOU'RE IN THE THICK OF THINGS!
AND "IN THE THICK OF THINGS" IS WHERE MOST WOLFRIDERS TEND TO LIVE!
THAT'S CERTAIN! NOW... FOR THE DARK STUFF! JUST REMEMBER...
...DREAMS NEVER HAPPEN NOW!

"YOU **BOTH** SAW THE FOREST **SHRINK**. REDLANCE WAS THE HELPLESS **FATHER TREE**, DESTROYED BY HUMANS WITH **METAL** TOOLS AND WEAPONS!

"AND TREESTUMP WAS POWERLESS TO KEEP HIS **OWN** METAL WEAPONS FROM **KILLING** WHAT HE LOVES MOST!"

YOU ALL SHARE A KNOWING ABOUT THINGS LONG LOST... LIKE THE HOLT.
NIGHT-FALL AND TREESTUMP'S DREAMS WARN--
"--THAT SOME OF US MAY BE AS MUCH TO BLAME AS THE HUMANS IF WE LOSE IT AGAIN!
"BUT THEN, IF YOU THINK ABOUT IT, ALL OUR DREAMS ARE ABOUT THINGS CLOSING IN ON US.
"STRONGBOW AND MOONSHADE KNOW DEEPEST...FORGIVING-- AND LETTING BE--IS SOMETIMES ALL WE CAN DO."

THEN, MY DREAM--OF THE PIT--THOUGH IT'S DIFFERENT FROM MEMORY...IS TRUE?
ALL DREAMS ARE TRUE...EVEN ONES THAT SEEM BACK-WARDS FROM WHAT REALLY HAPPENS!
THE "KNOWING" IN US KNOWS ALL SIDES!
SO, WHAT IF DREAM TIME SPILLS INTO AWAKE TIME?
YEAH! HOW COME HALF OF US HAD GOOD DREAMS, AND THE OTHER HALF BAD?
Hmmm... WELL, HALF OF US CAN LIVE FOREVER!
"THE HALF THAT CAN'T HAS FEAR-DREAMS--SORT OF LIKE 'KEEP ALIVE' PRACTICE."
BUT THOSE LIKE PIKE AND TYLEET, WHO THINK AS IMMORTALS, ARE SIMPLY FREE OF FEAR.
THINGS DIE, THEY'RE REBORN AND THEY DIE AGAIN IN ENDLESS TURNINGS.
I THINK OUR DREAMS SAY NOTHING LASTS FOREVER --EXCEPT SPIRIT.
HIGH ONE...

WOLFRIDERS! WE'RE AWAKE! WE KNOW WHAT WE KNOW!
THE WORLD HAS CHANGED, AND OUR SMALL, GREEN PATCH OF IT WILL GET SMALLER!
BUT THERE'S POWER IN KNOWING! IF THIS HOLT FALLS, WE WON'T!
ON MY HEART I SWEAR THERE WILL ALWAYS BE A FATHER TREE, HERE, NOW, AND IN OUR DREAMS!
OOO WWOOOOOO

REMEMBER THIS, KITLINGS. ***THIS*** IS THE STRENGTH YOU COME FROM.
AND THAT IS YOUR SIRE, WHO LOVED US... AND NEVER FORGOT US... FOR ***EIGHT EIGHTS*** TIMES ***EIGHT*** TURNS OF SEASON.
DAWN'S FIRST, THIN RAYS DELICATELY SPECKLE THE TOWERING TREES OF ***THORNY MOUNTAIN HOLT.***
THE FOREST AWAKENS TO A CHORUS OF BIRDSONG AND THE CHATTER OF SMALL, FURRY SEED-SEEKERS.
WITH THE WOODLAND DAY'S ORDINARY BUSINESS BEGUN, THE COUNCIL OF WOLFRIDERS ENDS...

GLAD YOU STUCK TO IT, SQUIRREL-CHEEKS!
UM, Heh Heh...
A NEW KIND OF HEALING! I'VE LEARNED MUCH!
YOU MUST HELP PIKE ***KEEP*** ALL OUR DREAMS FROM NOW ON, AROREE...

"...AND YOURS TOO, FOR YOU SHALL HAVE DREAMS OF YOUR OWN AGAIN, I ***PROMISE!"***
WHO'D EVER GUESS ***PIKE*** WOULD COME UP WITH A GAME THAT WOULD WEAR OUT OUR ***THINK-MUSCLES?!***
Yawn ...EYES WON'T STAY ***OPEN!***

"BET NO FEAR-DREAMS COME CALLING ON US WHEN WE'RE THIS TIRED!"
AAAAAAAAAAAAAAAAH!
gasp
ONE...
...TWO...
...THREE...
...FOUR...
"ALL DREAMS ARE TRUE...THE KNOWING IN US KNOWS ALL SIDES!" WHAT THE WOLF CHIEF KNOWS IS THAT THE DREAM-GAME IS OVER-- FOR EVERYONE BUT HIM.

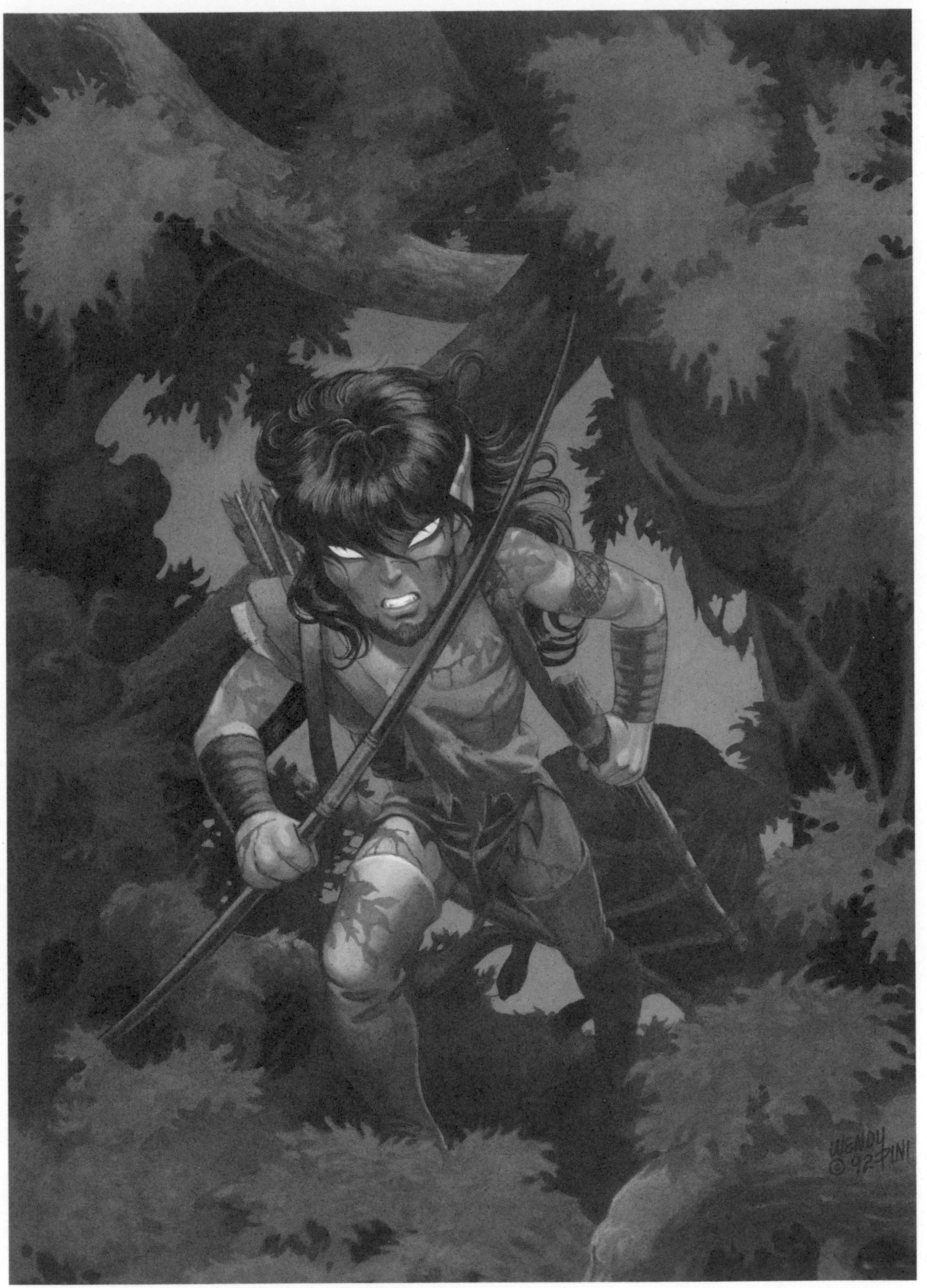

ElfQuest: Hidden Years *#1—"Wolfwood," originally published May 1992.*

ElfQuest: Hidden Years #2—*"Going Back," originally published July 1992.*

ElfQuest: Hidden Years #3—*"Little Patch," originally published October 1992.*

ElfQuest: Hidden Years #4—*"Right of Passage," originally published November 1992.*

ElfQuest: Hidden Years #5—*"Starfall, Starrise," originally published January 1993.*

ElfQuest: Hidden Years *#8—"Daughter's Day," originally published July 1993.*

ElfQuest: Hidden Years #9—*"The Enemy's Face," originally published September 1993.*

ElfQuest: Hidden Years *#9½—"Rogue's Challenge," originally published November 1993.*

BRODY'S GHOST™

CREATED BY
MARK CRILLEY

Brody hoped it was just a hallucination. But the teenaged ghostly girl who'd come face to face with him in the middle of a busy city street was all too real. And now she was back, telling him she needed his help in hunting down a dangerous killer, and that he must undergo training from the spirit of a centuries-old samurai to unlock his hidden supernatural powers.

Thirteen-time Eisner Award nominee Mark Crilley creates his most original and action-packed saga to date!

BOOK 1	BOOK 2	BOOK 3	BOOK 4	BOOK 5	BOOK 6
978-1-59582-521-6	978-1-59582-665-7	978-1-59582-862-0	978-1-61655-129-2	978-1-61655-460-6	978-1-61655-461-3
$6.99	$6.99	$6.99	$6.99	$7.99	$7.99

DarkHorse.com

AVAILABLE AT YOUR LOCAL COMICS SHOP OR BOOKSTORE To find a comics shop in your area, call 1-888-266-4226
For more information or to order direct: • On the web: DarkHorse.com
E-mail: mailorder@darkhorse.com • Phone: 1-800-862-0052 Mon.–Fri. 9 AM to 5 PM Pacific Time.